W9-BMU-944

CATHOLIC AND CHRISTIAN FOR YOUNG ADULTS

CATHOLIC AND CHRISTIAN
FOR YOUNG ADULTS

Questions and Answers
About the Faith

ALAN SCHRECK

SERVANT
BOOKS

PUBLISHED BY ST. ANTHONY MESSENGER PRESS
CINCINNATI, OHIO

RESCRIPT

In accord with the *Code of Canon Law,* I hereby grant my permission to publish *Catholic and Christian for Young Adults* by Alan Schreck.

Monsignor Kurt H. Kemo
Vicar General
of the Diocese of Steubenville
Steubenville, Ohio
May 23, 2007

The permission to publish is a declaration that a book or pamphlet is considered to be free from doctrinal or moral error. It is not implied that those who have granted the permission to publish agree with the contents, opinions or statements expressed.

Cover design by Brian Fowler, www.DesignTeamInc.com
Cover photo by Kushnirov Avraham/Dreamstime.com
Book design by Phillips Robinette, O.F.M.

LIBRARY OF CONGRESS CATALOGING-IN-PUBLICATION DATA

Schreck, Alan.
  Catholic and Christian for young adults : questions and answers about
the faith / by Alan Schreck.
      p. cm.
  Includes index.
  ISBN 978-0-86716-602-6 (pbk. : alk. paper) 1. Catholic Church—
Apologetic works. I. Title.

BX1752.S4 2007
230'.2—dc22

                      2007018575

ISBN 978-0-86716-602-6

Published by Servant Books, an imprint of
St. Anthony Messenger Press
28 W. Liberty St.
Cincinnati, OH 45202
www.AmericanCatholic.org

Printed in the United States of America.
Printed on acid-free paper.

07 08 09 10 11 5 4 3 2 1

Contents

Introduction

I post a warning here before you begin to consider this material: Thinking required!

This is a book especially for those who have questions about the Catholic faith—or about life—and who want answers. On the other hand, this book might raise some questions that you never thought about asking but (hopefully) will find interesting. Please note that this is not a complete catechism of Catholic beliefs; rather it discusses Catholic beliefs and teachings that are commonly misunderstood.[1]

Socrates once said that an unexamined life is not worth living.[2] At some point you will begin to ask yourself (if you haven't already) why you are alive, what is worth living for, what you believe about God and what you want to do with your life. Now, some people avoid considering these realities, subduing inner questions with a din of constant activity and video and audio amusements. But it is good, healthy and even important to slow down, quiet down and take time to think about the really important questions of life—and about faith. My hope is that this book will help you do just that.

If you're the type who likes to pick up a book and plow through to the end, be warned that you might find it easier to do that with a novel than with this book. This material might be easier to digest if you read just a few questions at a time and then think about the answers.

I suggest you also pray about the things you read here. Ask God to send the Holy Spirit to help you understand what you read and find the answers you need for your life. God loves you and is with you. He never turns away or ignores anyone who seeks him with a sincere heart!

Chapter One

God and Man

One of life's basic questions is, how did I get here? Indeed, why does anything (or everything) exist?

One explanation is that there is a Creator who brought everything into being. How can we find out if this is true? And if there is a Creator, what is this Creator like, and what is this Creator's relationship to the creation—and to us as part of creation?

Let's begin by looking at how people who think there is a Creator arrived at this conclusion.

Is there a God?

The first thing Christians say in their creed (their summary of essential beliefs) is, "I believe [*credo*] in God" or "in one God [*unum Deum*]."[1] Christians believe that God is the Supreme Being, the Creator of heaven and earth and everything that is. God does not make things out of something else, as a carpenter crafts a chair out of wood. God the Creator brings all things into being out of nothing. This is not magic. God simply is the Creator, and he has the power to do this. Jesus, the Son of God, demonstrated this same divine power when he fed five thousand people with a few fish and barley loaves (see Mark 6:30–44).

Is it reasonable to believe in God?

Some people think that those who have faith in God are irrational, accepting something that doesn't make sense. Or they think that those who believe in God are escaping reality by making up the existence of an invisible, spiritual world where God rules.

Belief in God is actually very reasonable, even if science can't prove it, because God's existence explains much about reality. If we ask one of the most basic questions, "Where did everything come from?" is it more reasonable to say, "Matter just appeared out of nowhere," or, "God—who is eternal, all-powerful and supremely intelligent—created the universe"?

Many philosophers, Saint Thomas Aquinas among them, have reasoned that there must be an original cause or source of the universe that produced matter, set everything in motion and ordered the universe according to so-called laws of nature, which are simply descriptions of the ways matter, energy, time, space and so forth act and interact. This first cause of all things and designer of the universe we call God.

Beyond this are invisible realities, such as love and goodness. Where does love come from—*love* meaning the desire to do good to others unselfishly? From where do we get the sense that love is good and noble if not from God, who is love (see 1 John 4:8)?

And what about the moral sense that humans have? We consider certain things to be fair or unfair in playing a game, and we assume that it is good to play fairly and wrong to break the rules of the game. Again, where does this sense of fairness come from if not from God?

A sign is something that points to something else. The

existence of an ordered universe, the laws of nature, a universal sense that there is right and wrong (like the "law of fair play"), the beauty of the world and so on are signs that point to the existence of an author, source and creator—that is, to God.

Why can't we see God?

There are those who say they can't believe in God because they can't see him, find him with their other four senses or run a scientific experiment to prove his existence. One of the first Russian cosmonauts proudly announced when he arrived in space that God and heaven were nowhere to be found.

J.B. Philips wrote a book called *Your God Is Too Small* (New York: MacMillan, 1967). His title is an apt commentary on this type of thinking. If God is the creator of all things, what makes anyone think that he is someone we can discern with any of our five senses or by means of scientific experiment?

God belongs to an entirely different order of reality that is not material and that is beyond space and time. The term Christians use for this different type or way of being is *spirit*. God is the one unlimited, eternal, all-powerful and supreme Spirit, the source of all other spirits (such as angels) and of the whole material universe. Everything that is not God is God's creation—creatures God has brought into existence.[2]

Perhaps you are wondering about where Christians get this idea of "spirit." In the Gospel of Saint John, Jesus explains to a Samaritan woman that "God is spirit, and those who worship him must worship in spirit and truth" (John 4:24). Also, Saint Paul taught that although God is the supreme spirit, he is not far away but is always present to us. Paul affirms what some Greek poets wrote: "In him we live and move and have our being" (Acts 17:28).

A second way to answer the question about where we can locate or find God is to consider another aspect of God—and a most important one: the fact that "God is love" (1 John 4:8). This means that God doesn't just love: God *is* love. God is the source of all love, just as God is the source of everything good. (More on this later!)

Christians believe that God created all things out of love, and he loves the whole creation. God created human beings out of love, and because we are capable of love, God created us to love him in return and to love each other as he loves us. Our greatest fulfillment as human beings, what makes us most like God, is the ability to love.

If God is the source of all things, what about evil? How can a God who is all-powerful, loving and all good allow evil to exist?

Since it is evident that there is evil in the world, it can seem that either (1) God is not totally good, if he is the source or cause of this evil, or (2) God is not almighty and in control of everything. But there is another option: God is all good and almighty but allows evil to exist.

At this point someone might ask for a definition of *evil*. It is true that some things that seem evil are not really so. For instance, earthquakes, hurricanes and other natural disasters that cause human suffering are not evil in themselves. Nonetheless, there are plenty of things that are plainly evil, such as the slaughter of the innocent in war and other sufferings unjustly imposed on innocent people.

Christianity and Judaism agree on the origin of evil.

Some of God's highest creatures—angels who possessed great intelligence, power and free will—abused their freedom, acting as if they were God by setting their own standards of right and wrong and choosing to serve and to honor themselves rather than the Creator. The irony is that this took place because of God's generosity. God blessed the highest creatures with attributes that reflect his image and likeness, such as power, intelligence and free choice. Yet this very freedom allowed these creatures to attempt to take the place of God and to rebel against his goodness and love. Pride was the root of their vice.

Jews and Christians call evil that comes from the choices of free and intelligent creatures against God—and against the order God created—by a particular name: sin. This rebellion against God and against the true meaning of right and wrong (God's moral law) is doomed to failure, because only God's truth and dominion will last. Only God, who created everything and holds it in being, is the "beginning and the end" (Revelation 21:6). Ultimately no creature, power or kingdom can stand against God, even though one of these may appear for a time to succeed or even to triumph.

How do we know that good will triumph over evil?

The last book of the Bible, the book of Revelation, gives us a glimpse of the final battle between the angels loyal to God and the angel who initially rebelled against God, who is referred to as a dragon:

> Now war arose in heaven, Michael and his angels fighting against the dragon; and the dragon and his angels fought, but they were defeated and there was no longer any place for them in heaven. And the great dragon was

5

> thrown down, that ancient serpent, who is called the
> Devil and Satan, the deceiver of the whole world—he
> was thrown down to the earth, and his angels were
> thrown down with him. (Revelation 12:7–9)

Chapter twenty of the book of Revelation tells us that
Satan and his allies will be "thrown into the lake of fire
and brimstone where...they will be tormented day and
night for ever and ever" (Revelation 20:10). This is the final
destiny of Satan and his minions. God's love and power will
ultimately overcome evil in all its forms.

Why doesn't God destroy all evil and punish all evildoers now?

There seem to be two answers.

One is that God loves all creatures, even those who
rebel and reject God's goodness. Human beings exist in
time and have the opportunity to change their minds,
repent and return to loving and obeying God. Saint Peter
wrote, "The Lord is not slow about his promise...but is forbearing toward you, not wishing that any should perish,
but that all should reach repentance" (2 Peter 3:9). Indeed,
God "desires all...to be saved and to come to the knowledge of the truth" (1 Timothy 2:4).

The other answer is that God respects the God-given
freedom of the higher creatures to choose, even when they
choose evil. They, for their part, must accept the consequences of their choices, even if it means total and eternal
separation from God, which the Judeo-Christian tradition
calls hell. More about hell in chapter ten.

If there is a God, why have people lost a natural sense or knowledge of him?

God created the human race in his image and likeness. What a great thing it is that God created us with intelligence and free will—freedom to choose—which are aspects of God's own nature!

Realizing that humans could choose evil instead of good, God promised that as long as humans continued to do good and to follow God's will, they would remain in close communion with him, knowing and loving God in a deep, personal relationship. However, the very first humans used their freedom to reject God and the true good. Instead they obeyed and followed the evil that God had warned against.

Have you ever experienced how mistrust and sin can damage or even break a relationship? Sin broke the close communion and loving relationship that God had intended for the human race. Put simply, humans abused their freedom, rebelling against God and choosing to follow their own ways. As a result, their knowledge of God became darkened and confused, and they began to create, follow and worship their own false gods.

How and when did this rebellion against God begin in human history?

The Bible tells us of two important or "original" instances of choices that shaped the destiny of the human race. The first was the rebellion—the refusal to love and serve—of some of God's highest creatures, the fallen angels, led by Satan, whom we also call the devil or "the evil one." This choice began the cosmic battle between the all-good God and the forces of evil, the eternal spirits who oppose him.

The second choice that affected human destiny came from this rebellious archangel's first appearance in human history, as recorded in the Bible's first book, Genesis. Satan, in the form of a serpent—"that ancient serpent" (Revelation 12:9)—tempted the first human beings and led them to rebel against God. Through their own free choice, Adam and Eve chose to disobey God. This is the original sin of the human race.

What were the results of original sin for the human race?

The major consequence of the evil choice of humanity's first parents was that Adam and Eve and all their offspring were separated from God and deprived of many gifts that God wished them to possess. Adam and Eve in their original state knew God personally and intimately (see Genesis 2); we, however, are born into the world not knowing God directly or naturally. This is a result of Adam and Eve's sin, also known as the Fall.

Some people have raised questions about the historical reliability of the creation accounts of the book of Genesis. On the one hand, there are those who claim that these accounts have no historical reliability: There never was an Adam and Eve or any original sin. On the other hand, some claim that the accounts must be taken absolutely literally as history: The first sin was the eating of a piece of fruit that God had forbidden.

The Catholic Church affirms that there were two first humans, each having a body and an immortal soul infused by God, and that they did disobey God's command to them through a willful and serious act—the original sin. The *Catechism of the Catholic Church* states: "The account of the fall in *Genesis* 3 uses figurative language, but affirms a primeval event, a deed that took place *at the beginning of the history of man* [Cf. *GS* 13§1]" (*CCC,* 390).

The *original sin* of Adam and Eve resulted in the loss of the original *innocence* and *righteousness* of the whole human race. Another effect of the original sin is that we are not inclined always to do good but often to do evil. This tendency is called "concupiscence."

We see the struggle between good and evil and confusion about what is good and what is evil not only outside of us but also within us. The result is that the human race needed—and needs—to be saved from this condition of sin and separation from God.

Who is God "in human form"? Why did God come to us in this way?

We have seen that God is a spirit and thus cannot be found through our human senses or by a scientific experiment. However, because God loves human beings and has created us to return this love, we have to be able to find and to know God in some way. Because God knows that it is difficult for human beings to love someone they can't see or touch, God had a remarkable and surprising plan: to take human form so that humans could see and touch him, could encounter God, who is spirit and pure, perfect Love.

Christianity is all about the person of Jesus, who is God in human form. Much more will be said about Jesus of Nazareth in this book, but this is the most important: Jesus is God incarnate—that is, God in the flesh. Jesus is "the image of the invisible God,...[and] in him all the fulness of God was pleased to dwell" (Colossians 1:15, 19)

Jesus is the one way that God has chosen to save humans from the consequences of original sin. Jesus is not just a great man or great moral teacher or a martyr for a cause. Jesus is the almighty, eternal God, who about two thousand years ago entered into human history. He is a divine Person born a man, of Mary of Nazareth in Bethlehem. God sent Jesus to heal the division between God and humanity—to save the human race from all sin and its effects.

Don't Christians exaggerate the importance of Jesus by making him into God?

It is nearly impossible to say too much about Jesus or to overemphasize his importance. Christians take their name from Jesus Christ. It should be considered an honor to be called a "Jesus fanatic" or something similar. Christians through the centuries willingly and joyfully have shed their blood and given their lives simply because they refused to be quiet about Jesus or to deny that he is God in the flesh.

There is no danger of making Jesus into God, for Jesus *is* God. He is the fullness of God's love, power and wisdom made visible. As Saint Paul said, "Christ the power of God and the wisdom of God" (1 Corinthians 1:24).

Jesus is also humanity's Savior—the God who took human form to deliver our race from the bondage of sin. If you are searching for God and wondering if God exists or what God is like, Christians simply will tell you, "If you truly know Jesus, you have found God and know what God is like."

What do Christians mean by having faith in God or in Jesus?

The Letter to the Hebrews, in the New Testament, says that "faith is the assurance of things hoped for, the conviction of things not seen" (11:1).

As we have said, God is spirit: Human eyes cannot see him, nor can our senses know him. Since God is not material, no instrument or experiment can detect his presence. *Faith* or *belief* in God and in Jesus is the *conviction* that God is real and that he sent his only Son Jesus to be our Redeemer.

We might say of a close friend, "I believe that he or she loves me." We cannot see or measure the person's love, but we judge by what we can see, such as how the person acts toward us. We could be right or wrong, but it is reasonable to believe in a person's love for us if the signs point to it.

When Christians say that we have faith in God or believe God exists, we are convinced by various signs that God exists and that we can put our trust and hope in him and in his goodness and love. Likewise, when Christians say that we believe or have faith in Jesus, we profess that he is not just a man who lived two thousand years ago but also God incarnate—God in the flesh. Various signs or indicators convince us that this is true.

Faith in God and in Jesus is different from faith in other things in one important way: Believing in God (and all that God wants us to know) is so essential to our life and destiny that this faith is a gift—something that God enables us to do or to have. So if a person is struggling to believe in God or to believe that Jesus is truly God (as well as fully human), he or she can ask God for the gift of faith.

The prayer (words addressed to God) asking for faith may sound strange, but it is honest and it works: "God, I don't even know whether you exist, but I want to know the truth about you. If you are there, please help me to find you and to know you. Please give me faith to believe in you."

A person can make a similar prayer to Jesus if he or she is struggling to believe that Jesus is truly God and to accept Jesus as the Savior. How Jesus saves humanity from sin, death and separation from God is the subject of our next chapter.

Chapter Two

Salvation: God's Free Gift in Jesus Christ

Sometimes we find ourselves in a predicament from which we can't escape. We feel helpless or cornered, and we realize that we need help to get out of the situation in a good, positive way. We need to be saved.

Whether we fully understand it or not, the human race is in such a predicament. The first humans, Adam and Eve, rebelled against the Creator and caused the human race to become separated from God and inclined toward evil. We find ourselves in the situation that Saint Paul described:

> I do not understand my own actions. For I do not do what I want, but I do the very thing I hate.... I can will what is right, but I cannot do it. For I do not do the good I want, but the evil I do not want is what I do. Now if I do what I do not want, it is no longer I that do it, but sin which dwells within me.... Wretched man that I am! Who will deliver me from this body of death? (Romans 7:15, 18–20, 24).

If you can relate to this, read on!

Is there any way to come to know and love God once again?

God created humans out of love; he intended them to live in a relationship of love and communion with him. The all-knowing God knew that the human race would turn away through sin. He prepared a way, a plan, to draw the human race back into the loving relationship that we were created to enjoy. This is an expression of God's mercy, God's loving forgiveness or forgiving love. This love pardons all offenses and sins.

The overcoming of the broken relationship between God and the human race caused by original sin and every sin after that has a name: salvation—being saved from sin and all its consequences. Salvation means that we can come to know God once again and enter into that loving relationship with God for which we were created. The ultimate meaning of salvation is that when we die, we will, through God's forgiveness and mercy, enter into the ever-lasting joy of communion with God forever, which Christians call "heaven." (There's more on heaven in chapter ten.) God's love is so great that it overcomes human sin and the physical, emotional and spiritual death that results from sin.

How does God save us from sin and bring humans back into loving communion with him?

God's work of saving the human race from sin unfolds in history. The whole story, which is the main subject of the Bible, is too long to be told here. In short, God formed a people—the Hebrew or Jewish people, the nation of Israel—and gradually revealed to them his identity and saving plan.

Although God's saving plan was obstructed by the sin and weakness of this people, God made it clear that it *would* ultimately succeed because it was *God's* work and plan. The faithful love of God for this chosen people, and through them for the whole human race, would not be thwarted, in spite of their unbelief and sinfulness. This is what God's plan was designed to overcome.

The climax of this divine plan was the sending of an anointed one, the Messiah, who would save the people of Israel and *all* peoples who would receive God's mercy as revealed in this Savior. It was through the Savior that all human sin would be forgiven and the human race reconciled with God.

Who is the Savior who would forgive all sin and enable all people to come back into a right relationship of love and friendship with God?

Christians believe that Jesus of Nazareth, who walked the earth two thousand years ago, is the Christ—the anointed one or Messiah—and the world's Savior. He is the only one who can bring any person fully into a right relationship with God, cleansed of all sin. As the Bible says of Jesus, "There is no other name under heaven...by which we must be saved" (Acts: 4:12).

Saint Paul described his own powerlessness to break from sin—"Wretched man that I am! Who will deliver me from this body of death?"—and immediately gave the answer: "Thanks be to God through Jesus Christ our Lord!" (Romans 7:24–25). Jesus is the one who saved Paul from his bondage to sin, and Jesus alone can save us too!

Where did this Jesus come from? Who is he? How did he enter human history?

Since this book is not a complete catechism, let's just briefly review the basic facts that Jesus taught his followers.

First, Jesus said that his Father, God, sent him into the world to call people to turn away from their sin—to repent—and to bring them back to friendship or communion with God. As Jesus put it, God's kingdom or reign was "at hand": It was breaking into the world. This happened whenever anyone accepted his message, his Good News or gospel.

Jesus identified himself as the only Son of God the Father, which means that Jesus also is God, sharing the same nature or being as God the Father. And Jesus said that he and his Father would send the Holy Spirit, pointing to a Third Person of God. It is only because of Jesus' teaching that the world has come to know the full truth about God: that the one God exists as a vibrant unity of three distinct Persons: the Father, the Son, and the Holy Spirit—the Blessed Trinity.

Since Jesus claimed to be the unique Son of God, sent into the world by God the Father, is Jesus a man, or is he God?

The answer is, both! Everything in the accounts of Jesus' life indicates that he was human. He ate, drank, slept, rejoiced, suffered and even died. Yet Jesus *must* be God. His power and wisdom and all that he did and taught in his earthly life point to this. He multiplied food, stilled storms, healed people and even raised dead people to life at a word or command.

There is one more thing Jesus did that everyone knew

only God could do: He claimed to forgive people of all their sins and make them pure and righteous before God. In short, he claimed to save them from all sin and evil and its consequences. Jesus came into the world to complete God's plan to save the human race from the sin that separates us from God's love. Ultimately he would do this by dying on the cross for us and rising from the dead.

Why did God's Son need to save humans from sin? Why couldn't a great human being have done this?

Even though it seems incredible, it makes sense that the only one who could forgive the human race of all its sins and evildoing and give humanity a new start is God. No human being (even a great one), nor any angel or spirit for that matter, has the right and the power to save humanity (or even one person) from sin and sin's consequences.

When God forgives our sin and our rebellion, we *are* reconciled with God. We can receive God's love once again and enter into the loving relationship for which we were created.

Why did God become human to save the human race from sin?

Logically, God didn't need to become human to forgive the human race. God is God, and he could have decreed from heaven: "I forgive all the rebellion and evil of the human race, and I declare everyone freed from sin and once again in my friendship."

Christians have given many explanations for why God became human in order to save the human race. One is that it is a matter of justice. It was the disobedience of a human being—Adam, the first man—that began the separation between God and humanity, so it is only just that a human being—Jesus, the new Adam—would make up for the offense, the sin, of the first man. As Saint Paul wrote: "Then as one man's trespass led to condemnation for all men, so one man's act of righteousness leads to acquittal and life for all men. For as by one man's disobedience many were made sinners, so by one man's obedience many will be made righteous" (Romans 5:18–19).

There is a deeper reason for God the Son's becoming human to save the human race. When the perfect, sinless one entered the world in order to save it, the people he had come to save rejected him. Though some stood by Jesus to the end, others turned him over to be mocked, scourged, tortured and put to a horrible death. By becoming human, God our Savior shows the real horror of sin: the blindness, hardness and hatred that sin has caused in human hearts. The sinless one visibly took the world's sin upon himself and showed the price that must be paid to free the world of this sin.

More importantly, however, God's becoming human shows the great, unbounded love that God has for his human creatures, that he would take on our human nature and share in our deepest suffering and pain in order to free us from it. Saint Paul reflects on this: "While we were yet helpless, at the right time Christ died for the ungodly. Why, one will hardly die for a righteous man—though perhaps for a good man one will dare even to die. But God shows his love for us in that while we were yet sinners Christ died for us" (Romans 5:6–8).

Ultimately this is the only convincing answer to the question posed in chapter one, "If God is a loving God, why does he permit evil and human suffering?" God does not *cause* the suffering that comes from human sin: That is the result of our own choices. God's answer is to take that suffering upon his own shoulders as a human being—to *suffer with us*—without bitterness toward the human race for the pain we have brought about through our sin. He does this with love and mercy and forgiveness.

The greatest mystery of the Christian religion is that God takes on our full humanity and, by suffering the full effects of sin, forgives all those who ever have sinned. God, as it were, reverses sin's consequences, bringing new life through the power of his love—a love that even conquers death, the worst and most fearful fruit of sin. "Christ has been raised from the dead, the firstfruits of those who have fallen asleep. For since death came through a human being, the resurrection of the dead came also through a human being. For just as in Adam all die, so too in Christ shall all be brought to life" (1 Corinthians 15:20–22, *NAB*).

This is not just a theory or a story; it has been accomplished. Jesus, the Son of God, really entered into history as a man. He was rejected; he suffered, died and rose from the dead after three days. Perhaps nowhere is this stated as beautifully as in Saint Paul's Letter to the Philippians, where he quotes an early Christian hymn:

Though he was in the form of God, [he] did not count equality with God a thing to be grasped, but emptied himself, taking the form of a servant, being born in the likeness of men. And being found in human form he humbled himself and became obedient unto death, even death on a cross. Therefore God has highly exalted him and bestowed on him the name which is above every name, that at the name of Jesus every knee should bow, in heaven and on earth and under the earth, and every

> tongue confess that Jesus Christ is Lord, to the glory of
> God the Father. (Philippians 2:6–11)

This is the "big picture" of who Jesus is and what he, as the Son of God, came into the world to do. There are some important specific questions about salvation, however, that should be considered here, especially since Catholics and other Christians sometimes have different beliefs regarding salvation and how we receive this great gift of God. Let's look at a few of these questions.

Is salvation a free gift from God, or is it something that a person needs to earn in some way?

The Bible passages I just quoted make it clear that God's plan to save the human race from sin and death—by the life, suffering and death of Jesus Christ—is a free gift that no human being deserves or can earn. "God shows his love for us in that while we were yet sinners Christ died for us" (Romans 5:8).

Like any gift, though, salvation needs to be received and accepted; and it can be refused. Jesus sometimes spoke about this in terms of entering into the kingdom or reign of God. We must allow God to rule over our lives in order to receive all the gifts God has for us, including freedom from sin and the eternal life that we call salvation.

How do we accept or receive God's free gift of salvation?

The Bible gives us a number of steps to take in order to say yes to God and receive his gift of salvation, and the Catholic Church affirms that they are all important.

1. The first step is *faith*. To accept God's gift of salvation, it is important that I believe in God and acknowledge that Jesus is the Savior of the world and the one who saves me. "For by grace you have been saved through faith; and this is not your own doing, it is the gift of God" (Ephesians 2:8). The Gospel of John tells us: "For God so loved the world that he gave his only-begotten Son, that whoever believes in him should not perish but have eternal life" (John 3:16). Some refer to this verse from John as the best short summary of the gospel, the Good News of Jesus Christ. It indicates that we must believe in Jesus to accept the gift of eternal life.

   Jesus said, "He who hears my word and believes him who sent me [God the Father], has eternal life; he does not come into judgment, but has passed from death to life" (John 5:24). And he told his apostles, "Go into all the world and preach the gospel to the whole creation. He who believes and is baptized will be saved; but he who does not believe will be condemned" (Mark 16:15–16; also see John 6:28–29; 11:25–27; 20:30–31; 2 Thessalonians 2:13).

2. *Baptism* is also a way that we say yes to God and accept God's gift of salvation. Throughout the Acts of the Apostles, whenever anyone came to believe in Jesus, the apostles baptized the person as Jesus had instructed them. Baptism is not just a symbolic ritual: it is a sacrament, a way that God gives the free gift of salvation and we receive it.

   In the Gospel of John, Jesus explains to Nicodemus, "Unless one is born of water and the

Spirit, he cannot enter the kingdom of God" (John 3:5). From the beginning of Christianity, the followers of Jesus understood that a person needs to be "born anew" by water and the Holy Spirit through baptism in order to receive God's gift of salvation and enter God's kingdom or reign.

3. Jesus gave the Church *other sacraments* by which we can receive the gift of salvation and eternal life. He gave his apostles the power to forgive sins in his name, which comes to us now in the sacrament of penance or reconciliation (see John 20:21–23; Matthew 16:19; 18:18). He also gave us his own presence in the Eucharist, a tremendous sacrament of salvation.

   Jesus explained the meaning and importance of the Eucharist, this great saving gift, at the Last Supper with his apostles the night before he died. In chapter seven we will explore the meaning of the Eucharist more fully; it is enough here to quote one line of Jesus' teaching on the Eucharist: "Unless you eat the flesh of the Son of man and drink his blood, you have no life in you; he who eats my flesh and drinks my blood has eternal life, and I will raise him up at the last day" (John 6:53–54). Catholics receive God's free gift of salvation when they receive the Body and Blood of Jesus in the sacrament of the Eucharist.

4. Finally, to say yes to the gift of salvation, it is necessary that we *obey God,* doing all that he commands. This is a matter not of earning salvation but of acknowledging that true faith in God, by

which we receive salvation, is more than a verbal yes to God or believing in God in our minds. If it is genuine faith, it is something we have to *live,* to put into action.

Saint James points out that "even the demons believe [in God]—and shudder" (James 2:19). The demons believe, but their belief is not true faith, because they do not love or obey God. Jesus warned, "Not everyone who says to me, 'Lord, Lord,' shall enter the kingdom of heaven, but he who does the will of my Father who is in heaven" (Matthew 7:21).

Catholics believe that true faith will express itself in the way the person lives. Saint James states, "Faith by itself, if it has no works, is dead" (James 2:17). The key to Jesus' teaching on how to live is to love God and neighbor. Love is the fulfillment of all of God's laws (see Romans 13:10). When we love as Jesus instructed us, we obey God and thus accept God's gift of salvation. Without love, which is really God's love in us, no one can be saved (Matthew 16:27; Romans 2:5–10; 2 Corinthians 5:10; James 2:14; 1 Peter 1:17).

In summary, we accept God's free gift of salvation by

1. faith, believing in Jesus as one's own Savior;

2. baptism, receiving the sacrament by which God gives the saving grace of Jesus Christ;

3. reception of the Eucharist, the sacrament of reconciliation and other sacraments by which God extends mercy and salvation;

4. obedience to God, especially observing the great commandments of loving God and one's neighbor.

All of these are specific ways, revealed in the sacred Scripture, that we say yes to God and receive the salvation God so longs to give us.

Is salvation something we can lose?

Some Christians have a "once saved, always saved" view. Catholics believe that salvation is a gift that we must *continue* to accept. Because we live in time, unlike angels and other purely spiritual beings, human beings normally are able to make free and responsible choices throughout their lives. It is possible for anyone—even an apparently good Christian—to reject God by renouncing belief or by committing serious sin, which separates a person from God.

Catholics find this view expressed many times in the Bible. In the Old Testament God puts before the people a choice of life, by obeying God's commands, or death, by rejecting them (see Deuteronomy 11:26–28; 28; 30:15–20). God speaks through the prophet Ezekiel:

> Have I any pleasure in the death of the wicked, says the Lord GOD, and not rather that he should turn from his way and live? But when a righteous man turns away from his righteousness and commits iniquity and does the same abominable things that the wicked man does, shall he live? None of the righteous deeds which he has done shall be remembered, for the sin he has committed, he shall die. (Ezekiel 18:23–24)

Is God's judgment unfair? Ezekiel says no (see 18:25–29). People are responsible for their choices and must live with the consequences.

Saint Paul said he refuses to judge himself (1 Corinthians 4:3–5) but focuses all his attention on "what lies ahead,...[pressing] on toward the goal for the prize of the upward call of God in Christ Jesus" (Philippians 3:13–14). Some people, it seems, fail to reach the goal. Judas, an apostle chosen by Jesus, betrayed his master and hung himself. Who would appear less likely to lose his salvation than one of the twelve apostles of Jesus?

On the other hand, sincere repentance for even the most grievous sin puts us back into right relationship with God. This can even be a "final hour" or "deathbed" repentance. Because of this the Catholic Church does not claim to know that any particular person is in hell, since any person could turn to God for mercy in the final moment of life.

The Catholic Church urges Christians to pray for the grace of final perseverance, the grace to keep following Jesus right up to the moment of death. Jesus himself says that the person "who endures to the end will be saved" (Matthew 10:22; Mark 13:13). As many a wise coach has said, "It's not so much how you start that counts but how you finish."

Do we know whether we will be saved? Should we worry about this?

Today I am inclined to say that people ought to be more concerned about their salvation than they are. Our society generally tells us to do what feels good or feels right, regardless of whether or not it *is* right. If you think that your choices and actions have no real eternal consequences, besides the effects they have on others, then perhaps you *should* be more concerned about eternal salvation.

When speaking about how to enter the kingdom of heaven, Jesus advised: "Enter by the narrow gate; for the gate is wide and the way is easy, that leads to destruction, and those who enter by it are many. For the gate is narrow and the way is hard, that leads to life, and those who find it are few" (Matthew 7:13–14).

This saying, I think, is meant to wake us up to reality. No one just drifts into heaven. Jesus said that we have to *decide* to follow in his path, and this means taking up our cross every day (see Luke 9:23). It's clear that entering the kingdom of God is not always easy; it involves sacrifice.

Back to our question, do we know whether we will be saved? If this means knowing absolutely that we will be saved, the answer is no. As Saint Paul said, he did not judge himself: God is the final judge of us all, and before a person's death, only God knows absolutely whether that person will be saved. (*After* they die is a different story, which we will consider in chapter eight.)

Remember that a righteous person can turn away from God through serious sin or unbelief up to the moment of death. To imagine that it is impossible for this to happen to us is a sin of pride called *presumption,* presuming that I am too good or holy to ever turn away from God. Saint Peter said, "Even though they all fall away, I will not," and, "If I must die with you, I will not deny you," and before the night was over, he denied knowing Jesus three times (see Mark 14:29–31). Peter was truly repentant, and Jesus forgave him for this sin.

Although we cannot be absolutely certain about our salvation, we can be hopeful and confident about it. The Bible teaches that if we have committed our lives to Jesus Christ and have decided to live in God's service, God gives us the virtue of hope. Hope is the confident assurance that, as we live in faith and in love, God will bring us into full, eternal union with him in heaven. Hope is a firm trust in God's love and mercy.

Already, Saint Paul says, the Holy Spirit has been given to us through faith and baptism and is a foretaste of heaven, the "first fruits" (Romans 8:23) of the salvation that Jesus has won for us. As Saint Paul wrote in the Letter to the Romans, "We rejoice in our hope of sharing the glory of God.... And hope does not disappoint us, because God's love has been poured into our hearts through the Holy Spirit who has been given to us" (Romans 5:2, 5).

To sum it up, if you dedicate yourself to following Jesus within his body, the Church, you don't need to worry or be concerned about whether you will be saved. The Holy Spirit—God himself—will give you hope and trust in God's love, which will not fail.

Is there any other Savior besides Jesus?

Have you ever heard the saying, "There are many ways to God"? It is a popular idea, and it usually means that it doesn't really matter whether one believes in Buddha, Allah, Confucius or Jesus. The idea is that nearly all religions, Christian and non-Christian, are equally valid ways of living a good life and finding and honoring the Supreme Being.

Christians don't believe that all ways to God are equal. In fact, although there are truths, even many truths, in religions other than Christianity, followers of those religions do not know or believe the most essential truth about God: that he so loved us that his Son became human, suffered and died to save us from sin. No other religion but Christianity believes this, and no other Savior but Jesus Christ has accomplished this.

If Christians are wrong about this, then Christianity is not just another equally valid way to God but a false religion based on a lie. But if the claims of Christianity are correct, then it is the one true religion, and Jesus is the one and only Savior and Lord of the human race.

The roots of Christianity are in Judaism, the Jewish religion, which holds that there is only one God. Christians believe that Jesus, the Son of God made man, has revealed this one God fully. Jesus did not say that he was *a* way to know and come to God. No, he said, "I am *the* way, and *the* truth, and *the* life; no one comes to the Father, but by me" (John 14:6, emphasis mine).

As Saint Peter said of Jesus: "There is salvation in no one else, for there is no other name under heaven given among men by which we must be saved" (Acts 4:12). Jesus, the Son of God, with the Father and the Holy Spirit are one God who is to be loved, served, worshiped and adored by all people.

Does this mean that only Catholics, or only Christians, are saved?

First, Catholics believe that Jesus Christ certainly saves Christians who are not Catholic. We will discuss the relationship between Catholics and other Christians in chapter three.

But what about people who do not believe that Jesus Christ is Savior or Lord? From what we have read in the Bible about the importance of faith, baptism and the other sacraments in receiving God's gift of salvation, it would *seem* that someone who does not believe in Christ or hasn't been baptized could not be saved. Yet what about those who have never heard the Good News or never really understood who Jesus is and what he taught? Wouldn't it be unjust if these millions of people had no hope of salvation?

Catholics understand that faith in Jesus Christ and being baptized into Christ and his Church are the normal way of salvation. But since God is just and salvation is God's free gift, the Catholic Church holds that salvation is possible for people who, through no fault of their own, have not yet come to know of or believe in Jesus as Savior and Lord. These people are searching for God and for the true religion, and they are striving to live a good life, as they understand this, by following their conscience (see Romans 2:12–16).

There are perhaps millions of people in the world in this category, people whom God loves and for whom Jesus Christ died. God "desires all men to be saved and to come to the knowledge of the truth" (1 Timothy 2:4), and he "is the Savior of all men, especially of those who believe" (1 Timothy 4:10).

In Saint Matthew's Gospel Jesus explains how he will judge the nations—that is, non-Jews, those outside of God's chosen people—at the Last Judgment of the world: Did they feed the hungry, give drink to the thirsty, clothe the naked and visit the sick and imprisoned? Those who did those things "to one of the least of these my brethren" did it for Christ, and they will be welcomed into God's kingdom (see Matthew 25:31–40).

Faith is not mentioned in this judgment account; it is assumed that people of the "nations"—those outside of the Church—do not know who Jesus is and hence do not believe in him. And yet Jesus saves them and gives them eternal life if they have treated others with mercy and compassion.

Jesus *is* the only Savior. He saves these people even if they never have heard of him or perhaps never understood the gospel message. When faith is not yet present or mature, love may be sufficient for receiving God's free gift of salvation.

If love and following one's conscience are enough for a non-Christian to be saved, why bother telling others about Jesus?

Why does anyone need to be a Christian if they can be saved without knowing Christ? First, it is far better to know Jesus than not to know him. He is the source of our life and salvation and the one who reveals the full truth about God and humanity.

Second, the human race is engaged in a spiritual battle between Satan and God, and Satan knows that it is far more difficult to be saved without knowing Jesus. Yes, non-Christians may be saved, but as the Catholic Church taught at the Second Vatican Council (1962–1965):

> Rather often men, deceived by the Evil One, have become caught up in futile reasoning and have exchanged the truth of God for a lie, serving the creature rather than the Creator (cf. Rom. 1:21, 25). Or some there are who, living and dying in a world without God, are subject to utter hopelessness. Consequently, to promote the glory of God and procure the salvation of all such men, and mindful of the command of the Lord, "Preach the gospel to every creature" (Mk. 16:16), the Church painstakingly fosters her missionary work. (Dogmatic Constitution on the Church, 16)[1]

In sum, it is possible for a person to be saved without faith in Christ, baptism and the other sacraments, but it is far more difficult. We must remember Jesus' command to us, his followers,

> Go therefore and make disciples of all nations, baptizing them in the name of the Father and of the Son and of the Holy Spirit, teaching them to observe all that I have commanded you. (Matthew 28:19–20)

What if someone asks me, "Have you been saved?"

This sometimes seems like a trick question for Catholics, designed to trip them up. Catholics don't always know what the person is asking. "Have you been baptized?" would be an easy question to answer, but as we have seen, initial faith and baptism are just the beginning of a lifelong journey of following Jesus Christ in faith, hope and love.

So what do Catholics say if asked, "Have you been saved?" The simple answer is yes, but the question itself requires a fuller explanation.

Regarding the *past*, it is right to say, "I have been saved," because Jesus Christ came into the world and died on the cross for our salvation and for the salvation of all people. Regarding the *present* a Catholic can say, "I am being saved," because the grace of God is at work now in our lives through the Holy Spirit. We are responding to Saint Paul's exhortation to "work out your own salvation with fear and trembling" (Philippians 2:12), and we can rejoice as we "are being changed into [Christ's] likeness from one degree of glory to another" (2 Corinthians 3:18).

But as to the *future*, a Catholic Christian would say, "I hope to be saved," because Catholics know that we must trust in the grace of God to enable us to persevere to the end and to win, like the saints, the crown of eternal life. "Blessed is the man who endures trial, for when he has stood the test he will receive the crown of life which God has promised to those who love him" (James 1:12).

So in answer to the question, "Have you been saved?" a Catholic can say, "Yes, I have been saved, and I hope with God's grace to persevere on the way of salvation until I meet the Lord face-to-face!"

Chapter Three

The Sources of Catholic Beliefs

The Bible is a collection of writings that together tell one dramatic story. It begins by telling us that all things came into existence through a Creator, God, who fashioned the heavens and the earth and formed human beings in his own image and likeness to rule over the whole physical world. God also created the human race for deep lasting communion with each other and with him, but the sin of the first humans disrupted this plan. This original sin caused a great rift between God and the human race.

The rest of the Bible recounts God's dealings with humanity as he sought to restore the break in communion with his people that human sin had caused. Specifically God called individuals and then a people, the Jewish people, to experience and enter into his saving plan.

The Bible also records prophetic messages that foretell the coming of a Messiah or Savior to establish the reign of God permanently—forever. The New Testament of the Bible proclaims that this Messiah, the Savior of all people, has come to earth and established God's kingdom, which will last on earth until human history ends. That Savior is Jesus, who not only reveals God's kingdom and how to enter it but also enables us to know who God is and the relationship we are to have with God.

All this addresses the question of where Catholic beliefs come from, but there are many questions that still can be asked. How do we know that the Bible is true? Is the Bible the only source of our knowledge of God? We will look at these and related questions in this chapter.

How do we know that the Bible, the collection of writings that present this great epic story, tells the truth about God and human life?

Catholics accept the Bible as true, first, because we share the same *faith* as the authors of the Bible. We believe that God has broken into human history and revealed to us his will and plan for the human race.

Second, the Bible is credible: It tells a historical story and interprets history in a way that fits together and makes sense. It presents a picture of God as one whose deepest desire is to form a people to live as his people in righteousness and truth and to receive God's blessings. There is no "proof" that the Bible is true, but the story it tells is consistent and makes sense. If a person approaches the Bible and the teaching of the Catholic Church with an open mind, that person will have a chance to discover their wisdom.

How do we know that the Bible tells the truth about Jesus? Isn't it incredible to believe, for example, that a man is also God?

The main sources about Jesus' life are the four Gospels of the New Testament: Matthew, Mark, Luke and John. Even though these are four different "portraits" of Jesus, it is clear that they are all describing the same person. The Gospels fit together and complement each other remarkably, a sign that they are telling the truth about a real, historical person.

The Gospels claim that Jesus did amazing things that only someone with supernatural powers (like God) could do: healing people at a word of command, stilling storms, multiplying food and even raising dead people to life. And this same Jesus taught with a wisdom and brilliance that amazed people and confounded everyone who tried to trip him up. Jesus claimed to know all about the kingdom of God and how to enter it. On top of that, he claimed to know God personally, calling him *Abba* ("Dad"), which no Jew had ever done or would ever dare to do.

Do the Gospels tell the truth about Jesus? Perhaps we should ask: If there wasn't a historical Jesus who did and said all these things, who could have made up this story and devised the wisdom that has amazed and attracted people for two thousand years?

Jesus' closest followers were a motley assortment of fishermen, good-hearted women, tax collectors, revolutionaries and a few other common people, none of whom had any influence or social status among the Jews or the Romans. And Jesus was only a carpenter's son, which led people to ask, when he started preaching and teaching, "'Where did this man get this wisdom and these mighty works? Is not this the carpenter's son?... Where then did this man get all this?' And they took offense at him" (Matthew 13:54–57).

One further thought: If Jesus' followers had devised this story to make a hero out of Jesus, why does the story climax with his being rejected by his own people, mocked, stripped, scourged, led out and nailed to a cross? Yes, then he rose from the dead, but the Gospels tell us that the followers of Jesus had a hard time believing Jesus really was alive again after they had seen him brutally tortured and killed (see Matthew 28:17; Mark 16:11; Luke 24:10–11; John 19:14).

If one is a reasonable person, it makes far more sense to believe that Jesus actually received his wisdom and power from God, his Father—and indeed was the only Son of God as he claimed—than to argue that Jesus' followers made up the story of Jesus and his teachings. This would include their claim that on the third day after Jesus' death his tomb was found empty and he appeared to them alive. That would have been the most incredible tale of all if they had made it up.

Like all the stories of God's mighty works and all his teaching throughout the Bible, the Gospels leave each of us with a choice. Do we believe that the story they tell is true? Since we were not there to witness any of these events firsthand, there is no way to prove the truth of the Bible. But likewise there is no way to disprove it. The Bible has power because it speaks to the human heart and mind with its truth. Its words "ring true."

How was the Good News about Jesus communicated in the first centuries after his death?

Imagine that you are a Jew on pilgrimage to Jerusalem, early in the fourth decade of the first century AD, on your way to offer sacrifice at the temple on the Feast of Weeks, or Pentecost. As you enter the city gates, you hear a commotion echoing down the narrow streets. Curious, you push your way through the gathering crowd to find a small group of men and women shouting excitedly from a balcony overlooking the street.

Though dressed plainly, as Galilean hill folk, these people appear to be speaking fluently in a number of languages, because people from many lands understand them. Moving closer, you hear them speaking in your own native tongue! A rough-looking, bearded man among them comes forward and says to the crowd: "Fellow Jews, and all of you who are in Jerusalem, let me explain this to you; listen carefully to what I say."

The speaker, of course, is the apostle Peter, and the commotion in the street follows the outpouring of the Holy Spirit on the day of Pentecost. The disciples are proclaiming the Good News of Jesus' death and resurrection, boldly and in public for the first time (see Acts 2).

With the coming of the Holy Spirit at Pentecost, the church of Jesus Christ was empowered to proclaim the news about Jesus and his kingdom to the ends of the earth. At first this message was not written down but was alive in the hearts and minds of Jesus' disciples, especially the twelve apostles. These twelve were trained to understand and teach Jesus' message as no others were, for Jesus had formed them for this task. They had learned by walking with him through times of trial and glory.

So from the beginning of Christianity, the teaching of Jesus' apostles was the most reliable source for the truth about him. This teaching was passed on by word of mouth from believer to believer, community to community. There was no need to write anything down, since people were accustomed to remembering important stories accurately. Besides, Jesus' followers expected that he might return at any moment to establish the fullness of his kingdom.

This passing on of the Good News by mouth is called "oral tradition." *Tradition* simply refers to something that is passed on or handed over from one person or group to another.

When Jesus did not return in glory from heaven after a number of years, a few of his followers, called evangelists, decided to collect and write down the sayings and events of Jesus' life in an orderly way (see Luke 1:1–4), so that nothing important about Jesus would be forgotten. These written traditions are called Gospels. Four of them—those of Matthew, Mark, Luke and John—were treasured by the Christian communities over the years as reliable and powerful accounts of the truth about Jesus and his teaching.

These communities, or local churches, also treasured certain letters written by the apostles or followers close to Jesus: letters by Saints Paul, James, Jude and John and one called the Letter to the Hebrews.

The Gospels—along with an extension of Saint Luke's Gospel called the Acts of the Apostles—the letters and another work attributed to John, the book of Revelation, came to be called the New Testament. It took a long time for the Church to agree on the list of official writings of the New Testament—that is, the canon of the New Testament. In fact, agreement wasn't reached until AD 397 at the Council of Carthage, almost four centuries after Jesus.

The "sacred Scriptures" first used by the followers of Christ are what Christians now call the Old Testament. The early Christians used a Greek edition of these Scriptures called the Septuagint. Christians call the writings of the Old Testament and the New Testament together the Bible, which means simply "the Book."

Who decided what writings were to be included in the Bible?

As we will discuss in chapter five, this decision was the task of the leaders of the early Christian communities. These men took the place of the apostles as leaders and teachers of Jesus' followers. Called "bishops," they were the ones who discussed and finally agreed on which writings were truly inspired by the Holy Spirit for all times and thus were to be included in the Bible.

It is interesting to note that Jesus never gave any instructions about what writings he wanted preserved. In fact, he never even told anyone to write down the things he said!

The bishops realized that it was important for them to agree on which writings told the full truth about Jesus and God's plan. They believed that it was God, specifically the Holy Spirit, who enabled them to discern which writings did this, since Jesus called the Holy Spirit "the Spirit of truth" (John 14:17; 16:13) who would guide his followers "into all the truth" (John 16:13) and call to mind all he had taught them.

Are these writings in the Bible the *only* way that Christians know the truth about God and God's will?

Here is where some Christians disagree. At the beginning of the sixteenth century, Martin Luther began teaching that Christian beliefs were to be based on the Bible *alone (sola scriptura)*. Before this both Catholic and Orthodox Christians, who had separated by the end of the eleventh century, believed that God's revelation of the full truth was *not* limited to the Bible. Their belief was that the Holy Spirit also inspired and guided other traditions—those things handed on by Christians. This would include the essential aspects of

- how Christians worship together (called liturgy— the work of God's people);

- moral teaching (issues concerning how Christians are to live);

- beliefs that were not directly taught or explained in the Bible;

- other important decisions made at universal gatherings of the bishops (ecumenical councils) about Christian beliefs, such as how to interpret certain things in the Bible.

For centuries the followers of Christ understood that the Spirit of truth could and did guide God's people into all truth in ways other than (but never contradicting) what was in the Bible. The body of unwritten truths that are valid for *all* times, people and places (just as the Bible is) is called *sacred Tradition* or sometimes just *Tradition*.

Note that even the Bible refers to these traditions. Saint Paul wrote in one of his earliest letters: "Therefore stand firm and hold fast to the traditions that you were taught, either by an oral statement or by a letter of ours" (2 Thessalonians 2:15, *NAB*). Yes, Saint Paul did teach that "all Scripture is inspired by God" (2 Timothy 3:16), meaning here the Old Testament, but Paul never said that *only* Scripture—the written revelation—is inspired by God.

Therefore, Catholics would say that the truth that God wishes to reveal to all people for their salvation is found both in sacred Scripture and in sacred Tradition, each of which God has entrusted to the people of the new covenant, the Church. In short, God didn't put saving truth, such as the truth about Jesus and how his followers are to live, just into a book. God entrusts the truth to a *people* with whom he is in a relationship.

Catholics consider the Bible to be the book of the Church and sacred Tradition to be the Church's way of life. The latter includes, as we saw above, worship, moral life and how to understand and *live* what God has revealed. Catholics call sacred Scripture and sacred Tradition together the word of God, God's truth revealed to God's people. This truth gives us life (see Deuteronomy 8:3; John 4:14) and draws us into a living relationship with our God—our loving Father, his Son and the Holy Spirit.

Do all Christians agree on which writings belong in the Bible?

Sadly, they do not. Up to the time of the Protestant Reformation in the sixteenth century, Christians had come to agree on which writings God truly inspired, the "canon" of the Bible. The Protestant reformers, however, generally went back to using a Hebrew version of the Old Testament that excluded certain writings that Catholics and Orthodox Christians considered inspired and part of the Bible. Hence a Catholic must be careful to purchase a Catholic edition of the Bible, which will include all of the books that Catholics hold to be inspired by God.

Who has the ability and the right or authority to correctly interpret and teach the word of God?

Even if Christians agree on which writings belong in the Bible or what is part of sacred Tradition, they do not always interpret these in the same way. Many divisions in Christianity have occurred over such disagreements.

Catholics believe that God wills there to be one, undivided community of Christians—one Church—that is united in its faith. As Saint Paul wrote, "There is one body and one Spirit,...one Lord, one faith, one baptism" (Ephesians 4:4–5). How can there be unity of faith, however, if every Christian has the authority to decide exactly what the Bible teaches, how the Christian community is to worship, what is moral or immoral and so on?

Now, there may be some room for differences of opinion on some issues, but certainly we cannot see "unity of faith" when there are disagreements that lead Christians to divide into different denominations and churches, which no longer worship together or agree on what is essential to Christianity.

Catholics believe that if God intends there to be a united Church, he provides a form of leadership to preserve this unity. The leaders must have the right and the authority to determine what the Bible and Tradition mean and how we are to live as Christians. Catholics believe that God has given his people such leaders and teachers.

Who are the leaders whom God uses to lead the Church in unity?

The Church's first leaders, whom Jesus personally formed and taught, were his closest followers, the apostles. When the apostles founded new communities of Christians, local churches, they appointed certain men (whom the New Testament calls "elders," meaning "leaders of the Church") to lead and to teach these churches. It appears that by the beginning of the second century AD (about seventy years after Jesus' death and resurrection), an elder called a bishop led each of the local churches.

The bishop was the spiritual father of the local church and its authoritative leader. Bishops often wrote letters to one another and sometimes met together to discuss issues that affected them all. They were especially concerned to maintain the unity of faith and practice.

In chapter five I will discuss how the leaders of the church emerged and worked together. For now it is enough to say that it is a matter of fact, not opinion, that from the time of Jesus' apostles to the present, there has been an unbroken line of leadership in the Church, and one of their key responsibilities has been to maintain the unity of the Catholic (universal) Church.

One way Church leaders have preserved unity is by proclaiming the gospel of Jesus Christ (as the apostles did) and teaching its true meaning. This service of teaching the truth is called the "magisterium" of the Church, from the Latin word *magister,* meaning "teacher."

How can we describe simply "where Catholic beliefs come from"?

An image or picture might help us. The Holy Spirit, the Spirit of truth, reveals the truth about God and his ways. Some of these eternal truths are written down (in sacred Scripture), and others are not—they are the lived truths of sacred Tradition. If we imagine the truths found in Scripture and Tradition as streams of life-giving water, these truths flow together into one stream in the life of the people of God, the Church. The magisterium, or teaching office of the Church, is like the streambed that guides the waters of God's truth along the right path—the way chosen by God and leading to the great sea of the completed kingdom of heaven that lies ahead.

I like this image because seeing truth as water reminds me of the life-giving water that the Bible so often uses as an image of refreshment for God's people. (In the Old Testament, for example, we have Psalm 46:4 and Ezekiel 47:1–10, 12.) Truth is refreshing and life-giving. The source of truth is God, and his truth comes to us through the inspiration of the Holy Spirit, the Spirit of truth.

Are you thirsty for the truth? Come to the Church, where the truth has been poured out in abundance and flows like living water from the source of truth, the Spirit of God, whom Jesus himself has sent. As the Gospel of John states: "On the last day of the feast, the great day, Jesus stood up and proclaimed: 'If any one thirst, let him come to me and drink. He who believes in me, as the Scripture has said, "Out of his heart shall flow rivers of living water."' Now this he said about the Spirit, which those who believed in him were to receive" (John 7:37–39).

There is another image of how God presents the saving truth that leads to salvation: envision a three-legged stool. The seat of the stool represents the truth; sacred Scripture, sacred Tradition and the magisterium of the Church are the three "legs," the three essential means of upholding God's revealed truth. As with any tripod, each leg is necessary.

Actually, I did not think of this image myself. The idea came from Vatican II's Dogmatic Constitution on Divine Revelation, which states:

> It is clear…that sacred tradition, sacred Scripture, and the teaching authority of the Church, in accord with God's most wise design, are so linked and joined together that one cannot stand without the others, and that all

together and each in its own way under the action of the one Holy Spirit contribute effectively to the salvation of souls (*Dei Verbum,* 10).[1]

In this chapter, then, we have seen the way that God has shown or revealed his truth and saving plan to the human race. Jesus called together a people from among both Jews and gentiles: all who believed he was the long-awaited Savior of the Hebrew people and of all humanity. He entrusted the truth about God and God's kingdom to his closest followers, the apostles, whom he sent out to teach others through the guidance of the Holy Spirit, the Spirit of truth. Eventually the teaching and life of Jesus took written form, and some of Jesus' closest followers wrote letters and other documents proclaiming and explaining the "Good News" about Jesus. The followers of Christ also passed on the way of life and worship they had received from Jesus in what was called "tradition," literally, those things "handed on." The leaders of the Church, the bishops (the apostles' successors) received from the apostles the role of teaching and interpreting with authority all that Jesus and the apostles taught, whether in written form or as living tradition. Thus the "Word of God" has been faithfully preserved and passed on to us today in forms of sacred Scripture (the Bible—the written "Word of God") and sacred Tradition (the Christian way of life—God's word as lived and practiced in the Church).

God's word, in these two forms, is treasured, proclaimed and authoritatively interpreted and applied today by the bishops, the apostles' successors including the successor or Saint Peter, the bishop of Rome, known as the pope.

Thanks be to God for providing such sure and reliable means of revealing and keeping truth that saves us and "sets us free" (see John 8:32)!

Chapter Four

The Church: God's Plan

If the goal of the Christian life is to get to heaven, why isn't it enough just to believe in Jesus and follow his teachings?

Many Christians have this "me and Jesus" approach to salvation and the Christian life. Catholics never would say that a person who did not belong to a church or see the importance of the Church could not be saved. The real question is, "What is God's plan?" Does God intend the followers of Christ to belong to a church or not? If so, what is the purpose of the Church in God's plan? Let's look at these questions.

Why do we need the Church?

It doesn't take a genius to figure out that the values that we find in the sacred Scripture—both God's commandments in the Old Testament and the teaching of Jesus in the New Testament—are under attack today. Sometimes the attack is subtle, like the mockery of Christianity and of Christian values we see in the media. The idea is clearly communicated, "Who would believe in that? It's so narrow-minded and uncool."

Or the attack is direct, like the Supreme Court decision *Roe v. Wade,* which legalized abortion, resulting in the slaughter of over forty-eight million innocent, unborn humans in America since 1973. Other direct attacks include laws that forbid displaying Christmas scenes or the Ten Commandments on public property.

This is one reason why we need the Church. If civil society ignores or mocks God's commandments and the values of the gospel of Jesus Christ, we need a strong community of believers to embrace, live and proclaim these values.

The Catholic Church has stood up boldly for Christian values, not compromising them or watering them down, even when they are not popular. In a "culture of death," the Catholic Church stands for life, from conception to natural death. In a self-centered society that sees sex as a means of self-gratification, entertainment and even a marketing gimmick, the Catholic Church proclaims the sacredness of sex, the necessity of chastity and marriage as a lifelong commitment between a man and a woman made possible by the grace of Jesus Christ. The Catholic Church condemns the evils of free sex, divorce, pornography and all forms of artificial contraception.

In a world of confusion and darkness, the Catholic Church stands for justice and equality for all people. The Church works toward an end to war and violence and seeks peaceful solutions to human problems and disputes among peoples and nations. Even though the Church is not perfect, and its members often fail to live up to the high values and moral code we profess, it stands as a beacon of light and of hope for those searching for the truth and a better way to live.

And many people are searching. Those who have followed the easy and permissive values that Western society increasingly promotes sooner or later discover the emptiness of materialism and selfishness. They often come to realize that the end result of adhering to these values is truly a culture of death and despair, a dead-end street.

Jesus knew that living according to his teaching would never be easy. But he also knew that his was the only way of life that would bring real peace and joy to the human heart and to the world. God created us to live according to his design, and Jesus knew this design and knew its importance. Jesus' followers, the Church, are to be a "light to the nations."[1] Recall Jesus' words: "You are the light of the world. A city set on a hill cannot be hidden. Nor do men light a lamp and put it under a bushel, but on a stand.... Let your light so shine before men, that they may see your good works and give glory to your Father who is in heaven" (Matthew 5:14–16).

We, the Church, are the light of the world, reflecting the light of Christ. Human beings need the support of others to live in the light of Christ. Jesus designed the Church to be this support for his followers.

Are youth important in the Church?

Jesus always valued children and young people. He told his disciples, "Let the children come to me" (Matthew 19:14). He spoke with a rich "young man" about how to enter God's kingdom (see Mathew 19:16–22).

Pope John Paul II emphasized the importance of young people in spreading the gospel throughout the world and being the future of the Church. The call to be witnesses to Christ is not just for adults: It begins with baptism, grows with confirmation and is constantly nourished by prayer, the Eucharist, Bible reading and sound Catholic teaching.

With these, teens and young adults will bear fruit and be a light of Christ to others.

Consider these words of Pope John Paul II in his apostolic letter At the Beginning of the New Millennium:

> If there is an image of the Jubilee of the Year 2000 that more than any other will live on in memory, it is surely the streams of young people with whom I was able to engage in a sort of very special dialogue, filled with mutual affection and deep understanding.... I saw them swarming through the city [of Rome], happy as young people should be, but also thoughtful, eager to pray, seeking "meaning" and true friendship.... Yet again, the young have shown themselves to be for Rome and for the Church *a special gift of the Spirit of God.* Sometimes when we look at the young, with the problems and weaknesses that characterize them in contemporary society, we tend to be pessimistic. The Jubilee of Young People, however, changed that, telling us that young people, whatever their possible ambiguities, have a profound longing for those genuine values which find their fullness in Christ. Is not Christ the secret of true freedom and profound joy of heart? Is not Christ the supreme friend and the teacher of all genuine friendship? If Christ is presented to young people as he really is, they experience him as an answer that is convincing and they can accept his message, even when it is demanding and bears the mark of the cross. For this reason, in response to their enthusiasm, I did not hesitate to ask them to make a radical choice of faith and life and present them with a stupendous task: to become "morning watchmen" (cf. Is 21:11–12) at the dawn of the new millennium. (*Novo Millennio Ineunte,* 9)[2]

The Church needs her young people—the "morning watchmen" of the new millennium!

What do Catholics mean by "the Church"? Where did this idea begin?

To understand what Catholics mean by "the Church," we need to look back to the unfolding of God's plan for saving the human race—that is, for bringing human beings back into a loving relationship with him after the original sin of Adam and Eve.

The writings of the Old Testament tell of how certain individuals experienced a call to believe in God and to obey God's commands. Noah built a great ark because he heard God tell him to do so. Abraham left his homeland and went wandering with his tribe, the Hebrew people, to seek a land where he believed God was calling him. Centuries later Moses sensed that God was calling him to lead the Hebrew people out of captivity in Egypt and back to the land that God had promised them. God raised up judges and then kings to govern this people and prophets to speak his word to them, especially when they strayed from the path and the laws that God had given them.

In short, the main theme of the Old Testament writings is that God approached individuals in order to form a *people* who would be bound to God by a covenant—a solemn agreement God initiated to establish a relationship of faithfulness and friendship between him and his people.

We learn much about God from the relationship between God and this chosen people. We see God's righteousness expressed, for example, in the commandments God gave to Moses, by which the people were expected to live. We also see God's mercy, as he chose this people in spite of their weaknesses and their failures to observe his commandments, even serving the false gods that other tribes worshiped. When God's people were unfaithful to

God, God remained faithful to them and to the covenant he had made with them.

God constantly forgave the sin and infidelity of the covenant people, the Jewish or Hebrew people (also known by the name of one of their founders, Israel). God stirred their hope by promising through the prophets a Messiah. The prophet Nathan, for example, foretold this in a prophecy to David, Israel's greatest king (see 2 Samuel 7:12–13). This Messiah would receive God's anointing, just as kings received an anointing with oil on being installed. This Messiah would free the people from all their enemies and establish a kingdom that would last forever.

Christians believe that this promise of a Messiah was fulfilled in the person of Jesus, who by his death and resurrection established an everlasting covenant between God and a people of the new covenant, a new Israel, which we call the Church. In the first or old covenant, one had to belong to the Hebrew people—that is, be a physical descendant of Abraham—to be a full member of God's people. In the new covenant one becomes a *spiritual* descendant of Abraham and, more importantly, an adopted son or daughter of God through faith and baptism. We saw this earlier in discussing how God saves people from sin and death.

In short, God's plan for the human race is to make it possible for *anyone* to belong to God's family, to God's own people. A person becomes part of that family by believing that Jesus is the Messiah, the Christ, the Savior of all people and one's own Savior, and by being baptized.

How does one enter the Church?

When one comes to believe that Jesus is Lord, Savior and the Son of God, that person becomes part of the Church through *baptism*. In baptism someone—usually a priest—pours water over the one to be baptized or immerses the person in water, saying, "I baptize you in the name of the Father, and of the Son and of the Holy Spirit." Baptism is the door by which a person enters into the life of Jesus Christ *and* of his Church. In chapter seven we will explore what baptism does.

Why does a person who believes in Jesus as Lord have to belong to the Church?

You *can't* have Jesus without the Church, because once you come to believe in Jesus as Lord and Savior, you become part of the people who also believe in Jesus. It is unthinkable (and was even more so in Old Testament times) that one could be a Jew or a Hebrew without being part of the Jewish or Hebrew people. Likewise it is or should be unthinkable that one could be a Christian without being part of the Christian people, the Church of Jesus Christ.

Saint Paul saw being baptized into Christ as becoming part of Christ, part of Christ's own body, the Church (see 1 Corinthians 12:13). Members of the Church belong to each other: "We, though many, are one body in Christ, and individually members one of another" (Romans 12:5).

In summary, nowhere in the Bible do we find the idea of a "Lone Ranger" Christian (or Jew) who just belongs to God and is not a part of God's covenant people. Being a Christian is not just a relationship between two people—you and God, or "me and Jesus." To believe in Jesus requires considering oneself a member of the people whom God has called together to belong to him in a special way as his covenant people.

One of my favorite passages from the Second Vatican Council is this: "It has pleased God...to make men holy and save them not merely as individuals without any mutual bonds, but by making them into a single people, a people which acknowledges Him in truth and serves Him in holiness" (Dogmatic Constitution on the Church, 9).[3]

Why do we call God's people or family "the Church"? What does the word *church* mean?

The word *church* comes from the Greek *ekklesia,* which literally means those "called out of." The idea is that through the message or Good News of Jesus, God calls people *out of* the world and *into* a new relationship with God and the life of God's people.

Is belonging to the Church a law—something we have to do?

Saint Peter wrote, "Once you were no people but now you are God's people; once you had not received mercy but now you have received mercy" (1 Peter 2:10).

Being part of God's people, the Church, is a gift. It is a great alternative to living an aimless life or a life centered on pleasure or self-fulfillment. The real joy in life is in giving ourselves, to others and to God, as Jesus did. That is where we find what life is all about.

The description of the life of the early Christians in Jerusalem—the first church—is a model and a challenge for the members of the Church today:

> And all who believed were together and had all things in common; and they sold their possessions and goods and distributed them to all, as any had need. And day by day, attending the temple [read "church" today] together and

breaking bread in their homes, they partook of food with glad and generous hearts, praising God and having favor with all the people. (Acts 2:44–47)

Although the specific ways of expressing generosity, prayer and community may be somewhat different today, belonging to the Church of Jesus Christ is still a wonderful thing and ought to be a reflection of our thanks to God for his many gifts of life and salvation. Remember the words of Jesus: "By this all men will know that you are my disciples, if you have love for one another" (John 13:35).

Yes, the Church is beautiful and impressive in many ways, but does a person *have* to be a member of the Church to be saved and to be a follower of Jesus?

Once again, you can't separate Jesus from his Church. Jesus knew that he would be dwelling on earth as a man for only a few short years. This is why he founded the Church as the place to meet him after he ascended to his Father in heaven.

How do we meet Jesus in the Church? The Church is the place where God's word is proclaimed, including the life and teaching of Jesus in the Gospels. Jesus is present in the sacraments, which the Church celebrates, especially the Holy Eucharist. The leaders of the Church represent Jesus in a special way by being ordained (empowered) to continue Jesus' ministry in the world. And of course, the Church itself is the community of the followers of Jesus. When Christians gather as God's people, the Church, one should be able to sense the presence of Jesus, "for where two or three are gathered in my name, there am I in the midst of them" (Matthew 18:20).

If one is a follower of Jesus Christ, it is both natural and necessary to be part of the people Jesus established, his followers, the Church. The Church is a great gift that Jesus gave us, where he can continue to meet us, to teach us, to nourish us by the sacraments and to encourage us to continue on our journey to God's kingdom.

Can a person who claims to be a Christian but rejects the Church be saved?

In the case of a Christian who does not understand why the Church is necessary but who seeks to follow the way of Jesus, the Catholic Church believes that he or she may be saved by faith and baptism, though the way is more difficult and uncertain. Without the nourishment of God's Word and sacraments and the regular support of believers who gather to worship God and to support each other, it is hard to persevere in following Christ to the end of one's life.

Humans are social beings; we are made for community. God knows that, and so he chose to save individuals by forming them into a people, a community. Belonging to the Church is thus not a choice or an option for followers of Christ. Vatican II's Dogmatic Constitution on the Church teaches:

> Basing itself on scripture and tradition, [the Church] teaches that the Church, a pilgrim now on earth, is necessary for salvation: the one Christ is mediator and the way of salvation; he is present to us in his body which is the Church. He himself explicitly asserted the necessity of faith and baptism (cf. Mk. 16:16; Jn. 3:5), and thereby affirmed...the necessity of the Church which men enter through baptism as through a door. Hence they could not be saved who, knowing that the Catholic Church was

founded as necessary by God through Christ, would refuse either to enter it, or to remain in it. (*Lumen Gentium,* 14)

Nonetheless God, in ways known only to him, can extend his saving power to those who are not visibly members of the Church. Saint Augustine, in his *Treatise on Baptism,* said that some persons would be saved who truly love God as far as they understand him, even if they are not formally members of the Catholic Church. On the other hand, Augustine warned his fellow Catholics that some baptized members of the Church would not be saved if they did not love God and live in charity toward others.[4] Church membership is a great help to an individual in attaining salvation, but it is never an automatic ticket to heaven.

How do I know which Church is really the one Jesus founded?

Statements known as *creeds* are the great summaries of the faith of Christians. In one of these, Christians say: "We believe in one, holy, catholic and apostolic church." These are the four marks that identify the Church Jesus founded. Let's look at them individually.

What do we mean when we say that the Church is *one*?

Jesus only founded one Church, one people. Throughout the Church's history, Christians have sought to preserve this unity. Tragically, over the course of time divisions have occurred, so Christians are no longer fully united with each other but belong to different churches, communities and groups.

Catholics believe that the unity that Christ intended can still be seen in the Catholic Church. Over a billion members worldwide hold common beliefs, recognize and submit to the same leaders and are nourished by the same sacraments. Of course, even this unity of the Catholic Church seems fragile and imperfect. Yet the unity Catholics do possess remains a powerful sign of God's work of calling together a people.

What do we mean when we say that the Church is *holy*?

Holy does not mean "perfect" or "sinless" but "consecrated to God" or "set apart for God." Jesus said, "I came not to call the righteous, but sinners" (Matthew 9:13). It may seem contradictory, but Jesus calls sinners (us) to belong to a special, holy people—that is, a people set apart to be God's own.

In this sense the Church is like a hospital where everyone is being healed. More specifically in the case of the Church, everyone is being remade into the image of Jesus Christ. This is a lifelong process for most of us, but it is only within a holy Church, a people set apart by God, that we sinners can be made holy! Saint Peter urges us:

> Like newborn infants, long for the pure spiritual milk, that by it you may grow up to salvation; for you have tasted the kindness of the Lord.
>
> Come to him, to that living stone, rejected by men but in God's sight chosen and precious; and like living stones be yourselves built into a spiritual house, to be a holy priesthood, to offer spiritual sacrifices acceptable to God through Jesus Christ.... [For] you are a chosen race, a royal priesthood, a holy nation, God's own people, that you may declare the wonderful deeds of him who called you out of darkness into his marvelous light. (1 Peter 2:2–5, 9)

Note that Saint Peter did not say that the "spiritual house" of the Church might, someday in the future, become holy. He said that "you *are*...a holy nation"! Holiness—being set apart for God—is not something the Church or any of us earns or deserves. Like salvation, it is a free gift of God. Holiness is both a call and a challenge.

Saint Peter wrote in the same letter: "As obedient children [of God], do not be conformed to the passions of your former ignorance, but as he who called you is holy, be holy yourselves in all your conduct; since it is written, 'You shall be holy, for I am holy'" (1 Peter 1:14–16).

Have you ever had someone tell you to act your age? That is, "You are X years old, so act like it!" Here the Lord is saying, through Saint Peter, "You *are* holy, part of my holy people by my grace, so act like it!" This should encourage us. Since God gives us grace, we can respond by being who we are: followers of Jesus Christ!

What do we mean when we say that the Church is *catholic*?

Catholic here means "universal" or "all-embracing." Jesus gave a final great commission to his followers before he ascended into heaven: "Go...and make disciples of all nations" (Matthew 28:19). Jesus invites everyone to belong to God's holy people, the Church.

The Church is not an exclusive club or sect, nor is it limited by the boundaries of language, race, culture or nationality. The Church is the means for the saving plan of God and the saving grace of Jesus Christ to reach all people everywhere.

Some people may be confused because this mark of the Church is also the name by which the largest united body of Christians calls itself: the Catholic Church. Actually, this name first came to be used as a proper name of Christ's Church in the second century, when small groups of people began to break off from the one, universal Church of Jesus Christ. They usually were called by the name of their leader: the Montanist church (after Montanus), the Novatianists (after Novatus), the Donatists (after Donatus). The one Church that they left simply called itself the catholic (universal) Church to distinguish itself from these groups that had broken away.

The name stuck. Saint Augustine, in the fourth century, wrote in his *Confessions* that his mother, Saint Monica, had earnestly desired that her son would become "a Catholic Christian" before she died. (Her prayer was answered!)[5]

This mark of being catholic certainly applies to the Catholic Church. It includes people of all the centuries since Christ established it. It embraces all cultures, races, languages and nations.

How is the church *apostolic*?

Saint Paul wrote that the Church is "built upon the foundation of the apostles and prophets, Christ Jesus himself being the cornerstone" (Ephesians 2:20). *Apostolic* has three meanings as a mark or characteristic of the Church, and they all refer to Jesus' apostles.

- *Apostolic* means, first, "missionary": the Church carries out the *mission* Jesus gave to the apostles to make disciples of all nations.

- Second, *apostolic* means "teaching what the apostles taught in the power and with the guidance of the

Holy Spirit." This is called "handing on the apostolic tradition"—the genuine teaching of the apostles.

- And third, *apostolic* means that the leadership of the Church includes the apostles and those leaders who succeeded them, the bishops, in an unbroken line. This unbroken line is called "apostolic succession."

Why is this mark of the Church important?

The apostolic nature of the Church confirms it as the one true Church. It also supports and builds the Church's unity.

In the first centuries there were groups who were very missionary but who did not follow the teaching or the succession of the apostles. One type of group claimed to have teachings that went beyond that of the apostles, including new sacred writings—new "gospels." The Church called these people "Gnostics." There were other groups who claimed that their leaders did not have to be true successors of the apostles. Their leaders, they claimed, were holier or had greater spiritual gifts than the bishops and other leaders (priests and deacons) who led the Church as successors of the apostles. How did the Church respond to these groups and their claims?

Regarding the "Gnostics," who claimed to have new revelation, the Church recalled the warning of Saint Paul: "I am astonished that you are so quickly deserting him who called you in the grace of Christ and turning to a different gospel.... But even if we, or an angel from heaven, should preach to you a gospel contrary to that which we preached to you, let him be accursed" (Galatians 1:6, 8).

In response to those who rejected the successors of the apostles, Saint Clement of Rome, the third pope, wrote a famous letter in AD 96 to the Church in Corinth, correcting them for breaking away from the true leaders of the Church. Saint Ignatius of Antioch wrote to churches on his way to being martyred in Rome in AD 107. He urged them to obey their bishop, priests and deacons in order to maintain the unity of the Church.[6]

As the history of the Church unfolded, many more groups broke its unity by claiming to have new revelations from God or by rejecting the leadership of the successors of the apostles, inventing their own church structures and leadership. But the apostolic Church, the Catholic Church founded on the apostles and their teaching and led by their successors, continued to flourish and maintained its unity, which is its first mark or attribute.

Why are some Catholics called "Roman Catholics," others "Byzantine Catholics" and so on?

The terms "Roman Catholic" and "Byzantine Catholic" refer to rites (liturgical and spiritual "families") within the Catholic Church. All of them trace their origins back to one of the churches founded by the apostles of Jesus or their immediate successors. For example, the Roman Catholic Church traces its beginnings to Saints Peter and Paul, who founded the local church in Rome and were martyred there.

Although there are some differences in the customs and liturgies of these different rites, their beliefs and the essential characteristics of their liturgies and practices are the same. All recognize the bishop of Rome, the pope, as the chief shepherd of the Church, are obedient to him and are in full communion (full unity) with him and with all Catholics of whatever rite.

The rites of the Catholic Church are branches of the Catholic Church's "family tree." They are all closely related, without any divisions that would prevent members of one rite from fully participating in the life and worship of another rite.

Much more could be said about the Church, and perhaps you have many more questions, some of which may be addressed in the following chapters. It is most important to remember that it is God's will to gather a people to be his own special people—fully united in love and faith and redeemed by Jesus Christ. The Church is a gift to each person.

Even leadership, with the authority to serve God's people, is a gift. This we will discuss in the next chapter.

Chapter Five

Leadership in the Church

The issue of authority is at the center of many of the arguments and divisions among Christians. Who has the right to lead the Church? Why not just let the Holy Spirit lead the Church instead of arguing over who's in charge?

Let's look first to Jesus, the founder of the Church, and to the Bible and Tradition to see if we can find the answers to these questions.

How did Jesus intend leadership in the Church to work?

Did Jesus provide leaders for his people, the Church? Certainly. Out of all his followers, Jesus chose twelve men—symbolizing the twelve tribes of Israel—and gave them special instruction and authority to carry on his mission after he departed. His plan was that these men would lead the Church, the community of his followers.

Jesus gave one of the twelve, the fisherman Simon, a new name: Peter, which means "rock." "I tell you, you are Peter, and on this rock I will build my Church, and the gates of Hades shall not prevail against it. I will give you the keys of the kingdom of heaven, and whatever you bind on earth shall be bound in heaven, and whatever you loose on earth shall be loosed in heaven" (Matthew 16:18–19).

At the end of Saint John's Gospel, Jesus tells this same Peter to "feed my sheep" (John 21:17). The Good Shepherd, Jesus, is giving a significant task to Peter and Peter alone.

Jesus gave all the apostles authority to "bind and loose" (see Matthew 18:18) and to forgive sins (John 20:21–23). He also commanded them to lead "all nations" to become his followers through baptism (Matthew 28:19). Jesus promised that those who believed in him would do even greater works than he did (John 14:12). The apostles certainly saw the fulfillment of this. "Many signs and wonders were done among the people by the hands of the apostles.... The people also gathered from the towns around Jerusalem, bringing the sick and those afflicted with unclean spirits, and they were all healed" (Acts 5:12, 16).

In short, Jesus set apart Peter and the apostles and the Holy Spirit anointed them as the first leaders of the Church.

Who had authority to lead the Church after the apostles or in addition to them?

Saint Paul explains that among the charisms or gifts the Holy Spirit gives the Church are the gifts of apostle, prophet and teacher. In fact, Saint Paul wrote that "*God has appointed*" these (1 Corinthian 12:28, emphasis added). This is sometimes called the "charismatic" leadership structure, because it is based on the charisms of the Holy Spirit.

The later New Testament letters 1 and 2 Timothy and Titus—the Pastoral Epistles—give the qualifications for the offices of bishop and deacon (see 1 Timothy 3:1–13;

Titus 1:5–9). It is especially important for the bishop to be "an apt teacher" (1 Timothy 3:2), because "he must hold firm to the sure word as taught, so that he may be able to give instruction in sound doctrine" (Titus 1:9).

The *Didache* (or *Teaching of the Twelve Apostles*) is an early Christian writing dating from around AD 100 to 110. This work indicates that there was a gradual transition from the leadership of the "charismatic" leaders (the apostles, prophets and teachers) to the "offices" of bishop and deacon.

> You must, then, elect for yourselves bishops and deacons who are a credit to the Lord, men who are gentle, generous, faithful, and well tried. For their ministry to you is identical with that of the prophets and teachers. You must not, therefore, despise them, for along with the prophets and teachers they enjoy a place of honor among you.[1]

At the beginning of the second century AD, the martyr-bishop Saint Ignatius of Antioch wrote letters to churches along his route toward Rome. In each of them he addressed *the* (single) bishop *(episcopos),* the presbyters or elders *(presbyteroi)* and the deacons *(diaconoi)* who led these particular local churches. He especially emphasized the fact that everyone would know they were following Jesus if they obeyed their bishop and these other leaders. For example, to the local church at Smyrna, Ignatius wrote:

> You should all follow the bishop as Jesus Christ did the Father. Follow, too, the presbytery as you would the apostles; and respect the deacons as you would God's law. Nobody must do anything that has to do with the Church without the bishop's approval. You should regard that Eucharist as valid which is celebrated either by the

bishop or by someone he authorizes. Where the bishop is present, there let the congregation gather, just as where Jesus Christ is, there is the Catholic Church. Without the bishop's supervision, no baptisms or love feasts are permitted. On the other hand, whatever he approves pleases God as well.[2]

Apparently then, by the second century the basic leadership structure or hierarchy of the local Christian church (later called a *diocese*) was established. The *bishop* had assumed the role of the first apostles as the chief teacher, evangelizer and liturgical leader of the local church.

The *presbyters* (also translated "elders") assisted the bishop. Soon afterward they were called "priests," since the role of a priest is to offer sacrifices to God, and one of their chief duties was to offer the sacrifice of the Mass when local churches grew too large for the bishop to preside over every eucharistic celebration. The title "priest" over time came to replace the title "presbyter."

Finally, the *deacons* handled practical matters, such as the distribution of food and money on behalf of the church (see Acts 6:1–6). They helped the bishop in other ways as well.

Today every Catholic "local church" or diocese is led by a bishop, a successor of the apostles, and by priests and deacons who assist him in the service of God's people. Even though some of the particular qualifications for selecting a bishop have changed from what the Pastoral Epistles prescribe, overall they are the same. The bishop is still the chief teacher, pastor and priest in each local church. He must be tested for this important role of successor to the apostles and special representative of Jesus Christ.

Saint Paul encouraged these officeholders to take their

responsibility of leadership very seriously. For example, he wrote to his disciple Timothy: "For this reason I remind you to rekindle the gift of God that is within you through the laying on of my hands; for God did not give us a spirit of timidity but a spirit of power and love and self-control" (2 Timothy 1:6–7).

What a great gift God has provided to the Church in leaders who guide, teach and serve!

What are the main responsibilities of bishops and priests?

Since bishops and priests represent Jesus, they carry on Jesus' own mission and ministry. This has three dimensions: Jesus is a priest ("a great high priest," Hebrews 4:14), a prophet greater than Moses (see Matthew 19:3–10) who taught about God on his own authority (Matthew 7:28–29) and "the good shepherd" who "lays down his life for the sheep" (John 10:11, 14–15) in guiding them to God's kingdom.

The Church sets apart bishops and priests (through the sacrament of holy orders, which I will describe in chapter seven) to continue Jesus' presence in the world as priests, prophets (teachers) and pastors ("good shepherds") of God's people. This is what we see them doing every day.

Why can't *any* Christian do what priests do?

It is true that all Christians share in some ways in the ministry of Jesus. We all are "a holy priesthood" called "to offer spiritual sacrifices acceptable to God through Jesus Christ" (1 Peter 2:5). We all are called to proclaim Jesus Christ and the truth he has taught and to care for others as does Christ the Good Shepherd.

However, Jesus chose the apostles to act in his name and with his authority, to represent him in a special way. Every human group needs leaders who are set apart and recognized by the group. The Church is no different.

Why do only males serve as bishops, priests and deacons in the Catholic Church?

Although Jesus had very close women followers, such as his mother, Mary Magdalene and Martha and Mary of Bethany, he selected and trained only men to lead his followers. No one has ever accused Jesus of being sexist. In fact, in his own time he was criticized for his openness in talking with women who were not part of the people of Israel, such as the Samaritan woman at the well (see John 4:1–42). He performed miracles at their request, such as the healing of the Syrophoenician woman's daughter (Mark 7:24–30). He forgave a woman caught in adultery— a sin punishable by stoning in Jewish law (John 8:3–11). He respected Martha and Mary of Bethany (Luke 10:38–42) and other women as companions in his ministry. And of course he honored his mother, Mary, and Catholics continue to hold her in the greatest honor after Jesus himself. She is truly "blessed...among women" (Luke 1:42).

Jesus could have selected women to lead his people, but he selected only men to do this. Because Jesus founded the Church, the Church believes it only has the right to follow Jesus' example. Orthodox Christians and many other Christian churches agree. In fact, for well over nineteen hundred years of Christianity, *no* major Christian body ordained women as bishops or priests.

One reason that Jesus may have selected men to lead is because of the symbolism of leadership in relation to the

Church. Christ is the Bridegroom, and the Church is his bride (see Ephesians 5:21–33; Revelation 21:2; 22:17). The leaders of the Church symbolize Christ, the Bridegroom, and they care for the bride, the Church. So it is appropriate that the overall leaders of the Church be male. Nonetheless, we will see that women, as well as men who are not ordained, have important leadership roles by word, example and service, with Jesus as their model and guide.

Does not being eligible for ordination deprive women of honor and authority?

The highest honor the Catholic Church gives is to declare a person a saint through the process called *canonization*. I haven't done an official count, but I would not be surprised if the Catholic Church has canonized more women than men. Some women have also been declared doctors of the Church—Saint Teresa of Avila, Saint Catherine of Siena and most recently Saint Thérèse of Lisieux—in recognition of their profound wisdom.

The quality that is most important in the Church—radically following Jesus Christ on the path of holiness—has nothing to do with gender. In fact, some of women's greatest natural strengths—such as receptivity, openness to others, compassion and the ability to nurture life—are attributes that can enable women to fulfill the great commandment of the Christian life: to love God and others.

To those who say that women are deprived of authority in the Church because they are not ordained, consider the moral authority of Blessed Mother Teresa of Calcutta; the prophetic authority of Saint Catherine of Siena, who told the pope to return to Rome or risk going to hell; and the authority of women such as Saints Scholastica, Jeanne

Françoise de Chantal and Elizabeth Ann Seton, who founded and headed communities of religious women that had enormous impact on the Church and civil society in their times.

We might also reflect on the authority that Jesus' mother, Mary, had in relationship to her son. Jesus was obedient to her not only as a child (see Luke 2:51) but also as an adult. Consider the wedding at Cana in Galilee: "When the wine failed, the mother of Jesus said to him, 'They have no wine.' And Jesus said to her, 'O woman, what have you to do with me? My hour has not yet come.' His mother said to the servants, 'Do whatever he tells you'" (John 2:3–5)

I think you know the rest of the story. Mary was never ordained and never led a church. But she had (and has) great authority in the kingdom of God.

What about the pope? Why do Catholics think that he has authority to lead and govern all Christians?

Jesus Christ is the Head of the Church. But Jesus knew that after he died, rose and ascended to the Father, his people, the Church, would need a head on earth to lead and guide them. When you look at human nature and consider human history, practically every great nation, empire or institution has needed a king, emperor, president, prime minister or CEO as the visible head. It is not surprising then that, before he left the earth, Jesus clearly singled out one man to head the apostles and the Church.

Jesus chose a natural spokesperson who always answered the critical questions. It was Peter who declared, "You are the Christ," when Jesus asked the apostles, "Who do you say that I am?" (Mark 8:29). And Peter would be the one to first announce publicly the news of Jesus' resurrection on the day of Pentecost (see Acts 2:14–35).

Jesus gave him the name Peter, or "rock," and said, "On this rock I will build my Church." Then he gave to Peter alone the "keys of the kingdom of heaven" (Matthew 16:18–19). In Luke's Gospel Jesus tells Peter that Satan would "sift you like wheat," but Jesus promises to pray for him "that your faith may not fail; and when you have turned again [after denying Christ], strengthen your brethren" (Luke 22:31–32). And in John's Gospel, Jesus' final conversation with Peter includes: "Feed my lambs," "Tend my sheep," "Feed my sheep" (John 21:15–19). Thus Jesus commissioned Peter to be the "good shepherd" who would feed and care for Jesus' flock after he departed.

Three Gospels, in different ways, tell us that Jesus gave Peter a special role in leading, strengthening or "shepherding" the Church in Jesus' name. And after Jesus ascended, the Acts of the Apostles confirms that Peter was, indeed, the head of the Church, working with the other apostles.

Was Peter to have a successor as head of the Church?

If Jesus wanted the Church to have an overall leader to be a focal point of unity, it makes sense that there would be someone to succeed Saint Peter after he died. Just as kings, emperors and presidents have successors to ensure stability and continuity in their countries, the Church would certainly have someone to succeed Peter as its recognized leader.

The question is, who? Peter was martyred in Rome, and so the bishop of Rome came to be recognized as the successor of Saint Peter, as the Church's "chief bishop."

The bishop of Rome eventually came to be called "the pope" (from *papa*) and "the Holy Father"—the Church's chief *papa* or father on earth.

As early as AD 96, Saint Clement, the fourth bishop of Rome, wrote a letter to the church at Corinth to settle a dispute over leadership. In the next century Pope Victor set a common date for the celebration of Easter. At the end of the second century, Saint Irenaeus of Lyons refuted false teachers by referring to "the tradition which that very great, oldest, and well-known Church, founded and established at Rome by those two most glorious apostles Peter and Paul." He went on to trace the succession of leaders of the Church from Peter to the twelfth bishop of Rome, who lived in his own time, Eleutherus. Irenaeus concluded, "Every church must be in harmony with this Church [in Rome] because of its outstanding pre-eminence."[3]

Later general (ecumenical) councils of bishops in the Eastern part of the Roman Empire would bring together mainly Eastern bishops. But these councils were not considered universal (for all Christians) unless the bishop of Rome had confirmed their teachings.

I could give many more examples, but the point is clear: Among all the leaders of the Church, the bishop of Rome was recognized as having a special place, a preeminence. He is the focal point of unity for the Church that Jesus founded.

Where do the pope, bishops, priests and deacons get their authority to lead: from God or from the people?

The authority of the pope, bishops and other ordained leaders of the Church—priests and deacons—does not come from the people, as in a democracy, but from God. Jesus chose Peter and the other apostles, and he gave them their authority. In the Acts of the Apostles, when people challenged the apostles about their authority to teach or lead or heal, the apostles explained that they did these things in the name—by the authority—of Jesus (see Acts 4:5–22). They prayed: "And now, Lord, look upon their threats, and grant to your servants to speak your word with all boldness while you stretch out your hand to heal, and signs and wonders are performed through the name of your holy servant Jesus" (Acts 4:29–30).

Jesus himself told the apostles when he was with them during his public ministry: "He who hears you hears me, and he who rejects you rejects me, and he who rejects me rejects him who sent me" (Luke 10:16). To hear the apostles is to hear Jesus, which is to hear God the Father.

I have heard that the bishops, and especially the pope, are infallible, that they teach without error. Is this true? How can a human being be infallible?

To answer this we must go back to Jesus' promise to guide his people, the Church, into "all truth" through the Holy Spirit. At his Last Supper with his apostles, Jesus said:

> I have yet many things to say to you, but you cannot bear them now. When the Spirit of truth comes, he will guide you into all the truth; for he will not speak on his own authority, but whatever he hears he will speak, and he will declare to you the things that are to come. He will glorify me, for he will take what is mine and declare it to you. (John 16:12–14)

The question is, *how* will Jesus guide his followers into "all truth" through the Holy Spirit, who declares all that Jesus taught and even "the things...to come"? Does each

Christian infallibly know all the truth through the Holy Spirit? That doesn't seem to be the case.

Christians who take this promise of Jesus seriously think that his words here are fulfilled in the teachers Jesus trained and sent out to proclaim the Good News—the apostles and their successors, the bishops. Surely the leaders Jesus established would receive the ability—the gift of the Holy Spirit—to teach and interpret the truth that Jesus sent them out to proclaim.

In the Church's experience, it is possible for an individual Christian or even an individual bishop to make a mistake about the truth that the Holy Spirit is revealing. However, there are three instances in which it appears that Jesus' promise about infallibility (teaching the sure truth by the Holy Spirit) is fulfilled. What are these?

First, if all Christians agree that something is true in the realm of religious belief, then surely the Holy Spirit had to inspire this agreement. Put another way, God will not allow Satan or worldly thinking to mislead the whole Church in a matter of faith or any truth that is important for salvation.

Second, if all the bishops of the Church, the successors of the apostles, agree on a truth regarding faith and salvation, surely the Holy Spirit is guiding them to teach the sure, infallible truth. The Catholic Church believes this is fulfilled when the bishops of the Church solemnly define a doctrine of faith and declare it to the Church and the world. This is usually done at an ecumenical council, when the bishops of the world gather together as the shepherds and teachers of the Church, asking the Holy Spirit, the Spirit of truth, to bless and guide their teaching and decisions.

Third, when the successor of Saint Peter, the pope,

solemnly defines and declares something regarding the Christian faith to be true, Catholics believe that the pope possesses a special grace of infallibility in this teaching. He represents Jesus Christ in a special way as the chief teacher and shepherd of the Church.

How can the pope teach "infallibly"?

Belief in the infallibility of a teaching of the pope is based, first of all, on the Bible's portrait of Peter. There were times when Peter was anointed by the Holy Spirit to proclaim a truth that God wished to reveal. At Caesarea Philippi Jesus asked the apostles, "Who do you say that I am?" Peter did not confer with the other apostles but was inspired by the Holy Spirit to say, "You are the Christ" (Mark 8:29).

The Acts of the Apostles recounts another revelation Peter received that was crucial for the life of the early Church and important for all later Christian history: The gentiles could be baptized without first being circumcised. Again Peter did not consult with anyone about this. The Holy Spirit led him to the house of the gentile Cornelius, where he understood the meaning of his vision and proceeded to baptize Cornelius and his household (see Acts 10).

These examples show that the Holy Spirit did, at times, give to Peter alone special guidance and revelation about Christian truth. Catholics believe that at certain times in Christian history, God has spoken similar words of sure truth through the pope, the successor of Peter. This infallibility in teaching Christian truth is a sheer gift or charism of God for the benefit of the Church; it has nothing to do with the natural wisdom, ability or virtue of the particular man who holds the office of pope.

We might also note that, just as Saint Peter did not always speak infallibly but sometimes spoke through an excess of zeal (see Matthew 14:28; Luke 22:33), the pope is not infallible in everything he says. Catholics respect the ordinary, everyday teaching of the pope because he is the chief teacher and shepherd of the Church, but only what the pope solemnly defines and then declares to be a doctrine of faith is considered infallible. It is also true that a doctrine that the pope repeats frequently and that has been taught consistently by past popes may also be regarded as infallible, even when not formally defined.

Only two of the pope's teachings in recent times have been considered infallible definitions of Christian faith: those of the Immaculate Conception of Mary (1854) and the Assumption of Mary into heaven (1950). These two doctrines will be discussed fully when we consider Catholic beliefs about Mary in chapter nine. They were defined not because they are the most important doctrines of the Catholic faith—ecumenical councils and other papal teachings had determined most of those long before—but because they were doctrines about which some Catholics were uncertain. Pope Pius IX in 1854 and Pope Pius XII in 1950 believed that the Holy Spirit had given them and the Church sufficient insight to formally define these beliefs as infallibly true.

The charism of infallibility is a great gift to the Church, whether it is expressed through the united teaching of the bishops, through the pope's defining or consistently teaching a doctrine under the anointing of the Holy Spirit or through the *sensus fidelium*—"the sense of the faithful" leading the whole Christian people. Catholic Christians believe that God uses all these channels to fulfill his promise to preserve his people in the truth until he comes again to reveal all truth in its fullness.

Why do Catholics give such honor to the pope? Doesn't this take away from the honor due to God alone?

The Bible frequently exhorts Christians to honor and respect the leaders of the Christian community (see 1 Thessalonians 5:12–13; 1 Timothy 5:17), and this would certainly include the pope. But the pope is not God, and Catholics do not honor him as God. Catholics respect the pope as the human representative, the vicar, of Christ Jesus. The pope is called "Holy Father" because he has a fatherly care for all God's people, like the good shepherd (John 10), and because his ministry reflects in an imperfect yet real way the care of God the Father for his people.

Most of all, Catholics respect the pope because they believe that God has given him a special gift to proclaim and defend the Word of God, as it has come to us in the Bible and authentic Christian tradition. Catholics believe that in respecting the pope and other Christian leaders, they are honoring God, who has raised these men up as leaders of his Church.

Catholic Christians rejoice before God that he has shown his love by using imperfect human beings to transmit and proclaim his perfect truth, which guides us to the Father through Jesus Christ and in the power of the Holy Spirit. We should remember the title that Pope Gregory the Great took for himself: "Servant of the Servants of God." The pope and all leaders of the Church are servants, like Jesus, who "came not to be served but to serve, and to

79

give his life as a ransom for many" (Mark 10:45). Jesus is the ultimate model and guide for leadership in the Catholic Church.

Chapter Six

The Work of the Holy Spirit

It is the Spirit that gives life" (John 6:63). We have spoken about the Church and its leadership, but now it is time to talk about how and why the Church exists. The Church is not a dead relic of past ages but is an alive and dynamic body. Why? The answer is, the Holy Spirit.

Who is the Holy Spirit?

Jesus taught that God is our Father and that Jesus is the Son of God, who came to reveal the Father and to lead us to the Father in God's eternal kingdom. "No one comes to the Father, but by me" (John 14:6). But who is this mysterious figure we call the Holy Spirit or the Spirit of God?

God *is* spirit—a nonmaterial being—but the term *Holy Spirit* refers to a particular Person of God, just as the Father and the Son are Persons. The Holy Spirit is the Third Person of God, making the one God a Blessed Trinity.

We would not know God as Father had not Jesus, his divine Son, become human to reveal him to us. Likewise, we would not know there is a Person called the Holy Spirit if Jesus had not told us about him. Jesus made it clear that the Holy Spirit is not just a force or a ghost but a person. In the Gospel of John, Jesus refers to the Holy Spirit as "another Counselor," or advocate, whom God the Father would send "to be with you for ever" (John 14:16), the "Spirit of truth" who "will guide you into all the truth; for he will not speak on his own authority, but whatever he hears he will speak.... He will glorify me, for he will take what is mine and declare it to you" (John 16:13–14). The Holy Spirit is clearly a Person who hears, guides and speaks.

The Holy Spirit glorifies Jesus. He was with Jesus during his public ministry, leading and anointing him. We read in the Gospel of Luke: "And Jesus, full of the Holy Spirit, returned from the Jordan, and was led by the Spirit for forty days in the wilderness" (Luke 4:1–2).

On his return to Nazareth, Jesus went to the synagogue and read this passage from the prophet Isaiah: "The Spirit of the Lord is upon me, because he has anointed me to preach good news to the poor" (Luke 4:18). Jesus added that these words were now fulfilled in him (see Luke 4:21).

Just as the Holy Spirit visibly came upon Jesus at his baptism in the Jordan River (see Luke 3:21–22), Jesus promised that *all* who follow him will receive the Holy Spirit as God's greatest gift: "If you then, who are evil, know how to give good gifts to your children, how much more will the heavenly Father give the Holy Spirit to those who ask him!" (Luke 11:13).

Jesus was the first great gift, the coming of God himself into our human condition to show the Father's love and to save us from our sin. The Holy Spirit's coming is also the coming of God himself, though invisibly, into our hearts. He comes to remake our human nature into the image of God.

The Holy Spirit comes to make us holy, as God is holy. This is called "sanctification," from the Latin word *sanctus,* meaning "holy." This work of making us holy—making us like God—is just one work among many of the Holy Spirit in the lives of the followers of Christ.

This explains why Jesus said, when his followers were troubled and sad after he told them he would be leaving them: "Nevertheless I tell you the truth: it is to your advantage that I go away, for if I do not go away, the Counselor [that is, the Holy Spirit] will not come to you; but if I go, I will send him to you" (John 16:7).

How do we receive this gift of the Holy Spirit, God coming to live within us?

Jesus told Nicodemus, "Unless one is born of water and the Spirit, he cannot enter the kingdom of God" (John 3:5). Nicodemus was confused, not understanding how a person who has been born once can be "born anew" of water and the Spirit. Jesus was referring to the sacrament of baptism, which cleanses a person of original sin, so that the Holy Spirit can come and make a home in the person.

As Saint Paul said, through baptism we become "temples" where the Holy Spirit dwells. "For by one Spirit we were all baptized into one body...and all were made to drink of one Spirit" (1 Corinthians 12:13; also see Ephesians 4:4–6). "Do you not know that your body is a temple of the Holy Spirit within you, which you have from God?" (1 Corinthians 6:19).

Jesus instructed the apostles to "make disciples" of all peoples by baptizing them in the name of the Father, and of the Son and of the Holy Spirit (see Matthew 28:19). Saint Peter began this task with the first public proclamation of the Good News on the day of Pentecost. When the people asked what they must do to become followers of

Jesus and receive the Holy Spirit, Peter said: "Repent, and be baptized every one of you in the name of Jesus Christ for the forgiveness of your sins; and you shall receive the gift of the Holy Spirit" (Acts 2:38).

Peter had just explained to the people that the great outpouring of the Holy Spirit that they were witnessing was a fulfillment of a prophecy by the Old Testament prophet Joel:

> And in the last days it shall be, God declares,
> that I will pour out my Spirit upon all flesh,
> and your sons and your daughters shall prophesy,
> and your young men shall see visions,
> and your old men shall dream dreams;
> yes, and on my menservants and my maidservants in
> those days
> I will pour out my Spirit....
> And it shall be that whoever calls on the name of the
> Lord shall be saved.
> (Acts 2:17–18, 21, quoting Joel 2:28–32)

Pentecost, the day God sent the Holy Spirit upon the Church in power, began the last days of the world: the age of the Church, which is marked by the sending of the Holy Spirit on all who believe in Jesus and are baptized.

What about the sacrament of confirmation? If the Holy Spirit comes at baptism, why do Catholics say that confirmation is the sacrament of the sending of the Holy Spirit?

Throughout the Acts of the Apostles, there are accounts of Jesus' followers announcing the good news of Jesus' resurrection by words and mighty deeds and baptizing those who came to believe. Sometimes we see the Holy Spirit come upon people first, and then they are baptized (see Acts 10:44–48). Sometimes people are baptized, and the Holy Spirit then comes upon them (Acts 2:38). But in either case it is clear that water baptism and the sending of the Holy Spirit go together.

From these and other passages from sacred Scripture, and from their experience of God's grace at work, the Church's leaders were able to see two movements of the Holy Spirit's coming to a person through the Church's official ministry. The first, as we have seen, is through baptism, in which Jesus' words to the Samaritan woman are fulfilled, "The water that I shall give him will become in him a spring of water welling up to eternal life" (John 4:14; also see John 7:37–39, in which the Holy Spirit is described as the "living water" flowing out of the heart of the person who believes). In this sending of the Spirit, the person becomes a "temple of the Holy Spirit," the place where the Holy Spirit dwells or makes a home. This is what makes a person a Christian, for where the Holy Spirit lives, so do Jesus and the Father (see John 14:15–24).

There is another way that the Holy Spirit comes to empower a person to live the life of Christ and to proclaim Jesus as Lord in word and deed. Jesus promised, "You shall receive power when the Holy Spirit has come upon you; and you shall be my witnesses...to the end of the earth" (Acts 1:8). Further, the Holy Spirit provides all sorts of gifts (*charisms,* in Greek) to enable the Christian to serve others and through these gifts to build up or strengthen the body of Christ, the Church (see Romans 12:4–8; 1 Corinthians 12; Ephesians 4:11–16).

The name *confirmation* is a good one for this action of the Holy Spirit, because the sacrament both confirms that the Holy Spirit is at work in a person's life and deepens and strengthens that work. The Holy Spirit confirms for that person that he or she belongs to Jesus Christ and is a full, active member of Jesus' Church, called to proclaim Jesus and to serve others in his name and power. See chapter seven for more about this sacrament.

What does the Holy Spirit do in the life of the Church?

The Holy Spirit is not just God's gift to the individual person, but as Saint Augustine said, the Holy Spirit is the "soul" of the Church, the source of its life and power.[1] There are various ways that the Holy Spirit works in the Church:

1. *The Spirit of truth.* The Holy Spirit guides the Church into all truth, as Jesus promised (see John 16:13). The Church's leaders receive a special gift of the Spirit to guard and proclaim the truth. This is a tremendous service to the people of God, protecting the Church from error and confusion.

   > And his gifts were that some should be apostles, some prophets, some evangelists, some pastors and teachers, to equip the saints for the work of ministry, for building up the body of Christ, until we all attain to the unity of the faith and of the knowledge of the Son of God. (Ephesians 4:11–13)

   > When you read this you can perceive my insight into the mystery of Christ, which was not made known to the sons of men in other generations as it has now been revealed to his holy apostles and prophets by the Spirit. (Ephesians 3:4–5)

2. *The Sanctifier.* One of the marks or characteristics of the Church, as expressed in chapter four, is that she is holy. The Holy Spirit is the source of the Church's holiness. The Church is not holy because she has better people than those outside the Church; no, the Church is holy because the Holy Spirit lives within her. The members of the Church are those "living stones" (1 Peter 2:5) who are being joined together and are growing "into a holy temple in the Lord; in whom you...are built into it for a dwelling place of God in the Spirit" (Ephesians 2:21–22). The Church's holiness is a gift of the Holy Spirit.

3. *The source of gifts for the body of Christ.* The Holy Spirit is not only a gift to the Church; he is the giver of gifts. Saint Paul in different writings (see Romans 12; 1 Corinthians 12; Ephesians 4) lists the variety of gifts that God bestows on individuals—not primarily for themselves but for the good of the Church. "To each is given the mani-festation of the Spirit for the common good" (1 Corinthians 12:7). The gifts of the Spirit are neither toys to amuse us nor trophies to be proud of: They are tools to build up and strengthen God's people.

   The variety of gifts is vast: teaching, prophecy, discernment, faith, healing, speaking in tongues, administrating, helping—even giving away money (see Romans 12:8)! In fact, Saint Paul doesn't even pretend to give a complete list, because the gifts God gives to individuals for the good of others and the Church are as unique as each person is. Saint

Paul seems to be saying, "Discover your gifts and then use them!"

4. *The Spirit of unity.* The Church is one, and the Holy Spirit is the divine source of that unity. The unity of the Church is not based on good feelings or on liking people in the Church, though we hope we will like some of them! And unity doesn't mean that members of the Church won't hurt or offend one another. If that were the case, Jesus would not have had to teach about forgiving "seventy times seven" times, nor would he have included "forgive us our trespasses as we forgive those who trespass against us" in the prayer he taught his followers (Matthew 18:22; 6:12).

What *does* unity mean? God is love, and the Holy Spirit is "God's love...poured into our hearts" (Romans 5:5). Saint Augustine described the Holy Spirit as the mutual love of the Father and the Son, and this love overflows to those who believe in and follow Christ, those who have received the Holy Spirit.[2] This love is not a feeling but a desire to serve and to put the interests of others before our own. Jesus went so far as to say "By this all men will know that you are my disciples, if you have love for one another" (John 13:35).

This love is a fruit of the Holy Spirit, whom God has given to us individually (see Galatians 5:22). It results in the fruit of unity in the Church. As Saint Paul said so beautifully:

> I therefore, a prisoner for the Lord, beg you to walk in a manner worthy of the calling to which

you have been called, with all lowliness and
meekness, with patience, forbearing [that is,
"putting up with"] one another in love, eager to
maintain the unity of the Spirit in the bond of
peace. (Ephesians 4:1–3)

What does the Holy Spirit do in the lives of individual Christians?

The images we have of the Holy Spirit as a dove, a mighty
wind and tongues of fire make it difficult to imagine him as
a person. Yet we must remember that Jesus called the Holy
Spirit a "counselor" (see John 14:16; 15:26). The Holy
Spirit is God living within us, and so I like to think of the
Holy Spirit as the divine friend closest to my heart.

Even though this is not exactly a biblical image, Saint
Cyril of Jerusalem taught in the fourth century: "The
Spirit comes with the tenderness of a true friend and pro-
tector to save, to heal, to teach, to counsel, to strengthen,
to console."[3] The *Catechism of the Catholic Church*
describes the Holy Spirit as "the interior Master of life
according to Christ, a gentle guest and friend who inspires,
guides, corrects, and strengthens this life" (*CCC*, 1697).

If we try to summarize what the Holy Spirit does (or
is meant to do) in the life of a Christian, we come up with
a summary of the whole Christian life. Life in Christ is
truly life in the Spirit. The Holy Spirit makes possible
everything God wants to do in us; the Holy Spirit makes us
truly alive.

To summarize this, I will list the works of the Holy
Spirit in the life of a Christian along with one or two
Scripture quotes relating to that work.

The Holy Spirit makes the Christian holy, forming him or her into the image of Christ. To live the way that Jesus taught is not easy. In fact, without the Holy Spirit it is impossible. The Holy Spirit is the new law written on the human heart (see Jeremiah 31:33–34), which makes the Christian "a new creation" in Christ (2 Corinthians 5:17). The Holy Spirit frees each person from the bondage of sin, which leads to death, and sets us free.

> Now the Lord is the Spirit, and where the Spirit of the Lord is, there is freedom. And we all, with unveiled face, beholding the glory of the Lord, are being changed into his likeness from one degree of glory to another; for this comes from the Lord who is the Spirit. (2 Corinthians 3:17–18)

2. *The Holy Spirit enables Christians to pray and to know God personally and experientially.* In order to pray you have to know God personally, and this is a work of the Holy Spirit. Only by the Holy Spirit can a person recognize and proclaim that Jesus is our Lord (see 1 Corinthians 12:3). The Spirit enables us to cry out to God as our dear Father, our *Abba* (see Romans 8:14–17; Galatians 4:4–6).

At one point Jesus "rejoiced in the Holy Spirit" and burst into a spontaneous prayer to his Father (Luke 10:21–22). The Acts of the Apostles records many similar instances in which the Holy Spirit came upon the followers of Jesus and inspired them to pray (see Acts 2:4; 4:23–31; 7:55–60; 10:44–46; 19:6). Prayer is a gift, a work of the Holy Spirit in us.

Someone once asked Pope John Paul II, "How—and for whom, for what—does the pope pray?"

He responded, "You would have to ask the Holy Spirit! The pope prays *as the Holy Spirit permits him to pray.*"[4]

John Paul II said about prayer: "The apostle [Paul] comes to the heart of the matter when he writes: '*The Spirit too comes to the aid of our weakness,* for we do not know how to pray as we ought, but the Spirit himself intercedes with inexpressible groanings' (cf. Rom 8:26)."[5]

Of course, Jesus also taught his followers to pray the Lord's Prayer, and he prayed the daily prayers of the Jewish people as well. There is nothing wrong with rote prayers, such as the rosary. The Holy Spirit enables these prayers to come from our hearts and not just from our lips.

3. *The Holy Spirit inspires a hunger for the truth.* The Holy Spirit brings freedom, and God's revelation is one way the Christian finds freedom. As Jesus said, "If you continue in my word, you are truly my disciples, and you will know the truth, and the truth will make you free" (John 8:31–32).

The Holy Spirit enables us to accept Scripture and the Church's teaching "not as the word of men but as what it really is, the word of God, which is at work in you believers" (1 Thessalonians 2:13). Christians can rejoice at this gift of truth and the hunger the Spirit puts in our hearts for it. Saint Paul quoted the prophet Isaiah in this regard:

As it is written,

> "What no eye has seen, nor ear heard,
> nor the heart of man conceived,
> what God has prepared for those who love
> him,"

God has revealed to us through the Spirit.
(1 Corinthians 2:9–10)

4. *The Holy Spirit gives the Christian boldness and wisdom in telling others about the faith.* This is called "evangelization." It means that we communicate our belief in Jesus and in our Catholic faith to others, in word and deed. The Bible makes it very clear that the Holy Spirit gives us the power to do this:

> You shall receive power when the Holy Spirit has come upon you; and you shall be my witnesses...to the end of the earth. (Acts 1:8)

> And when they had prayed, the place in which they were gathered together was shaken; and they were all filled with the Holy Spirit and spoke the word of God with boldness. (Acts 4:31)

> No one comprehends the thoughts of God except the Spirit of God. Now we have received not the spirit of the world, but the Spirit which is from God, that we might understand the gifts bestowed on us by God. And we impart this in words not taught by human wisdom but taught by the Spirit. (1 Corinthians 2:11–13)

5. *The Holy Spirit stirs up a desire for unity and fellowship.* By his very nature the Holy Spirit puts in the heart of each Christian a desire to be united with other followers of Christ.

Although some of us may have more independent personalities, we all need to give and receive spiritual support, support in the Holy Spirit.

> If we live by the Spirit, let us also walk by the Spirit. Let us have no self-conceit, no provoking of one another, no envy of one another....
>
> As we have opportunity let us do good to all men, especially to those who are of the household of faith. (Galatians 5:25–26; 6:10)

Pope John Paul II stated in January of 1993:

> Paul explained to us the nature of this fruit [of the Holy Spirit] in his Letter to the Galatians. It consists of "love, joy, peace, patience, kindness, generosity, faithfulness, gentleness, self-control" (Gal 5:22–23).
>
> The adoption of these interior dispositions, conforming the believer ever more closely to Christ, impels him towards an ever deeper communion with his brothers and sisters. Christ is indeed one, as is the Spirit who is the source of these interior dispositions. Therefore gifts charisms and virtues—when they are authentic—*tend concordantly and harmoniously toward unity*. In presenting this broad list of virtues, the Apostle significantly calls each of them "*the* fruit—*ho karpos*—of the Spirit": the various virtues, in their diversity, come together in the "one fruit" of the Spirit, which is love.
>
> St. Paul explains this to the first Christians of Rome: "The love of God has been poured out into our hearts through the Holy Spirit that has been given to us" (Rom 5:5). The love of God

> (*agape*) is shown by self-control and gentleness,
> in understanding for one's neighbour, in cordial
> relations and in a willingness to forgive....
>
> These are the essential prerequisites for
> truly seeking unity.[6]

Should we be able to know whether the Holy Spirit is alive and working in us and in the Church?

Even though the Holy Spirit is invisible, we can know his presence by his working in our life and in the Church. Are the fruits of the Spirit present: "love, joy, peace, patience, kindness, goodness, faithfulness, gentleness, self-control" (Galatians 5:22–23)? Are the gifts or charisms of the Spirit present? Do we use the Spirit's gifts to serve and encourage one another?

Are there unity, harmony and peace in the Church community? Is there a burning desire to tell others about the faith of Christ, to spread the Good News, to invite others into a relationship with Jesus and with his Church? Is there a hunger to know the truth: to study the Scripture and the teachings of the Church and to love and embrace these teachings?

Finally, do people have a personal knowledge of Jesus and the Father? Do they pray to God as someone they know and love as their Father?

If one can say yes to all or most of these questions, then it is clear that the Holy Spirit is present and at work!

Sadly, sometimes the Holy Spirit's work is stifled, either because of a lack of understanding or a wrong expectation of what the normal life of the Church should be like. For example, some people think that Christianity is all about keeping certain rules or attending a church service once a week—things that focus on external observances rather than on the "heart" where the Holy Spirit is at work.

Author Peter Kreeft comments on this state of affairs:

> When Paul visits the church in Ephesus (Acts 19), he notices something missing—I think he would notice exactly the same thing in most of our churches and preach the same sermon—and he asks them, "Did you receive the Holy Spirit when you believed?" (Acts 19:2). Why would he ask that unless he saw a power shortage? Why did twelve fishermen convert the world, and why are half a billion Christians unable to repeat the feat? The Spirit makes the difference.[7]

What do we do if the presence of the Holy Spirit seems to be weak or even missing in our lives or in the life of our local church? Can a Christian ask for more of the Holy Spirit—his presence and power—other than through the sacraments?

First, the Church *is* the "dwelling place of God in the Spirit" (Ephesians 2:22), and each baptized Christian is a temple of the Holy Spirit, a place where the Spirit lives (see 1 Corinthians 3:16–17; 6:19; 2 Corinthians 6:16). Saint Irenaeus said, "Where the Church is, there also is God's Spirit; where God's Spirit is, there is the Church and every grace [St. Irenaeus, *Adv. haeres.* 3, 24, 1:PG 7/1, 966]" (*CCC*, 797, quoting *Adversus Haereses,* 3, 24).

But sacred Scripture and Tradition also insist that Christians can and should ask God for more of the Holy Spirit. We also should ask that the work of the Holy Spirit be stirred up or rekindled in our lives and in the life of the Church. Saint Paul used the image of a fire that has grown cold being fanned into flame (see 2 Timothy 1:6–7).

In teaching about prayer, Jesus practically commanded his followers to ask for the Holy Spirit:

> And I tell you, Ask, and it will be given you; seek, and you will find; knock, and it will be opened to you. For every one who asks receives, and he who seeks finds, and to him who knocks it will be opened.... If you then, who are evil, know how to give good gifts to your children, how much more will the heavenly Father give the Holy Spirit to those who ask him! (Luke 11:9–10, 13)

An example of this type of prayer is in the Acts of the Apostles. After the Church had received the gift of the Spirit at Pentecost, the disciples gathered to pray for more boldness in proclaiming the Good News. What happened? "And when they had prayed, the place in which they were gathered together was shaken; and they were all filled with the Holy Spirit and spoke the word of God with boldness" (Acts 4:31). Ask, and you shall receive!

Jesus said, "It is not by measure that he [the Father] gives the Spirit" (John 3:34). God doesn't wish to give the Holy Spirit in a little measuring cup. He doesn't want to sprinkle the Holy Spirit; he doesn't want his followers just to wet their tongues with the living water. In the Gospel of Luke and the Acts of the Apostles, whenever Saint Luke speaks about God's sending of the Holy Spirit, he says that the Spirit is *poured* out, and those who receive the Spirit are all *filled* with the Holy Spirit (see, for example, Luke 1:41, 67; Acts 2:4, 17; 4:31; 9:17).

So what do Christians do if they detect a lack of presence of the Holy Spirit in their lives: inadequate knowledge of God and little desire to pray, to read Scripture, to tell others about Christ, to worship or to meet with other Christians for support? What if they encounter difficulty in loving others or in obeying God? What if they see a lack of the fruits of the Spirit? What if the gifts of the Spirit are not present or being used?

The answer is to ask God the Father and Jesus the Son of God for a fresh outpouring of the Holy Spirit, for a renewal of the grace of baptism and confirmation. Our recent popes John Paul II and Benedict XVI have recommended this, as well as the preacher to the papal household, Capuchin Father Raniero Cantalamessa.[8]

Millions of Catholics today can attest to the fact that God answers this prayer for the Holy Spirit when it is made fervently and persistently. Many renewal movements, such as the Catholic charismatic renewal, have spread throughout the Church, inspiring Catholics and other Christians to pray for a new outpouring of the Holy Spirit. As a result Pope John Paul II called this the era of a "new springtime" in the Church and the beginning of a "new evangelization," as Catholics are being filled with a new fervor to live and to proclaim the Gospel of Jesus Christ.[9]

As Saint Paul said, "The kingdom of God does not consist in talk but in power" (1 Corinthians 4:20). The Holy Spirit is the power of God that gives the Church the abundant life that Jesus promised (see John 10:10) and enables each Christian to live that life and to share it with others.

The Holy Spirit is also the principle of the Church's growth. Jesus compared the Church to a mustard seed—the smallest of all seeds that would grow into a large bush. The little band of Jesus' first followers did not look at all like the Church that emerged a century or a millennium (or two millennia) later. It was the Holy Spirit who guided and formed the Church at each stage of its development, just as Jesus nourished it with His own Body and Blood in the Eucharist (the subject of this book's next chapter).

Likewise, each Christian grows spiritually, and this too is the work of the Holy Spirit who lives within as the "growth principle" (the DNA of the soul) who enables us to grow up into the image of Jesus.

Through the Holy Spirit, "We all attain to the unity of the faith and of the knowledge of the Son of God, to mature manhood, to the measure of the stature of the fulness of Christ.... Speaking the truth in love, we are to grow up in every way into him who is the head, into Christ" (Ephesians 4:13, 15).

Chapter Seven

The Sacraments

Jesus is God incarnate, God "in the flesh." He walked the earth two thousand years ago, teaching with profound wisdom and performing powerful works: healing, deliverance, feeding multitudes, raising the dead. He truly demonstrated that the kingdom or reign of God was at hand—even in their midst.

Jesus no longer walks the earth physically, but his power and grace still are present in the world, especially through the Church he founded. Jesus promised: "He who believes in me will also do the works that I do; and greater works than these will he do, because I go to the Father" (John 14:12).

Jesus' promise to be with the Church always (see Matthew 28:20) finds fulfillment not only in the sending of the Holy Spirit but also in the Church's continuation of the ministry of Jesus through the sacraments. These are among those "greater works" that Jesus promised his Church would do, based upon his example, teaching and promises.

What are these sacraments? That is the topic of the present chapter.

From where do the sacraments of the Catholic Church come?

In God's plan to restore friendship between God and the human race, the Father sent his divine Son into the world to share in our struggles and the human condition. Jesus, as he walked among us, used normal human gestures and ordinary material objects as he performed works of grace and healing. These are the origins of what Catholics call sacraments—visible signs, such as objects and gestures, that confer God's grace.

Jesus blessed people and laid his hands on them to heal (see Mark 1:40–45); he breathed on the apostles to give them the Holy Spirit (John 20:22); he commanded them to baptize people (Matthew 28:19); he used bread and wine at the Last Supper to give them his own Body and Blood (Mark 14:22–25). Jesus even used his spit to open a blind man's eyes (Mark 8:22–26), though the Church did not adopt this as a sacramental sign!

In short, the sacraments come from Jesus.

Are the sacraments magic? Where do they get their power?

Sacraments are not magic; the signs and ceremonies that surround them do not have any power in themselves. The power of the sacraments comes from God through Jesus.

I like to envision the grace or power of the sacraments as streams flowing from the wounds of Jesus on the cross, channels of grace flowing down to the earth through the centuries and reaching us today. We might ask, "How do the acts of one person who lived two thousand years ago affect us directly today?"

Jesus intended what he did on earth to touch and bless

his followers for all times. The sacraments, all of them based on Jesus' words and example, were entrusted to his people, the Church, to make Jesus' power and love present. Even if he isn't with us today in a physical body, he is present—he continues to walk among us—with healing and blessing in the sacraments.

What is required of members of the Church in order to receive the grace of the sacraments?

Some sacraments have certain general requirements. Baptism, for example, is the first sacrament; it must be received before the others.

The one important thing necessary in order for a person to receive the full blessing and grace of any of the sacraments is faith: belief in Jesus and in the grace he wishes to give in the sacrament. We can see this in the life of Jesus. In almost every case where Jesus gave a blessing or performed a mighty work, a person first came to him in faith, not to test him to see whether he could do some sign.

Do the sacraments always work? What if someone receives a sacrament without believing in it, without faith?

The sacraments are sacraments of faith, requiring faith to unlock them and let God's grace flow freely. However, the Church performs the sacraments, and the Church believes in Jesus' words and promises. So whenever the appropriate person (usually a priest) performs a sacrament in the proper way (correct form), then the grace of the sacrament is present. Even if the person who gives the sacrament is in a state of sin, the grace of the sacrament depends on Jesus and the faith of the whole Church. Thank God that the sacraments don't depend on the ministers' virtue, since we are all sinners!

For example, Jesus is really present in the Eucharist whenever Mass is celebrated according to the norms of the Catholic Church. If a person goes up to receive Holy Communion but doesn't believe the Eucharist is Jesus (perhaps thinking it is just a piece of bread that reminds us of Jesus' Last Supper), he or she still truly receives Jesus.

However, a complete lack of faith in Jesus' presence in the Eucharist will not help the person grow closer to God and may even harm the person's relationship with God. Saint Paul warned that God will judge anyone who "eats the bread or drinks the cup of the Lord in an unworthy manner," such as without any belief or while living in a state of serious (mortal) sin, in rebellion against God. Such a person, Saint Paul says, "will be guilty of profaning the body and blood of the Lord," and "any one who eats and drinks without discerning the body [that is, without believing that this *is* Christ's Body] eats and drinks judgment upon himself" (1 Corinthians 11:27, 29).

The point is that receiving a sacrament is a serious and solemn event. It is approaching Jesus and humbly asking for and receiving his grace and blessing. The person who approaches Communion knowing that Jesus says it is his Body and Blood but without believing it, or while living in rebellion against God, is offending God.

Holy things, such as the sacraments, are not to be taken lightly or approached casually. Going to Mass is not like going to a movie. It is important that a person's heart be ready and prepared. The preparation is simple:

1. Turn from your sin. You must receive the sacrament of reconciliation or penance if you have sinned seriously or think you might have. Otherwise you can simply tell God you are sorry for any ways you have offended him or your neighbor before receiving the sacrament.

2. Tell God that you believe in the grace that the sacrament gives and that you wish to receive all its grace and blessing. It's that simple!

If a person is not sure that Jesus is really present in the Eucharist, that person still may receive the sacrament and ask God to *increase* faith, to help him or her believe more fully. Jesus sometimes chastised his followers—even his apostles—for their lack of faith or their little faith, but he wanted them to keep coming to him and following him so that their faith would grow.

The sacraments are sacraments of faith not only because they *require* faith but even more because they *nourish* faith: They help a person's faith (and hope and love) grow stronger. Jesus often said, "Come to me," or, "Follow me" (see Matthew 11:38; 3:19; 19:21). Christians respond to this invitation when they come to receive the sacraments.

What are the sacraments?

The Catholic Church recognizes seven sacraments: baptism, confirmation and Eucharist (the sacraments of initiation); reconciliation or penance and anointing of the sick (the sacraments of healing); marriage and holy orders (the sacraments of Christian vocation). All of these are based on a teaching of Jesus or something he did or commanded during his life on earth.

What is baptism?

We saw in chapter 2 that Jesus referred to baptism as being "born anew" or "born from above" by water and the Holy Spirit (see John 3:3–5) and that he commanded his followers to baptize (Matthew 28:19). Baptism is the *normal* way that one is saved (Mark 16:16) and enters into the life of God's people, the body of Christ, the Church (1 Corinthians 12:13). Saint Paul taught that we need to be "buried" in the waters of baptism in order to rise with Christ and have a new life of grace (Romans 6:3–11; see also Colossians 2:12). In the early Church the people who were baptized were clothed in white robes to signify their new life in Christ.

How does a person go about getting baptized?

In the first years of the Church, all you needed to do to be baptized was to express your belief in Jesus as Lord. Later the Church instituted more instruction (called "the catechumenate") so that those interested in becoming Christians could receive fuller instruction in the commandments and Christian life, in how to pray (learning the Our Father and other prayers), in the sacraments and in the fullness of Christian beliefs as expressed in the creeds, such as the Apostles' Creed and the Nicene Creed. This continues today in the Rite of Christian Initiation of Adults (RCIA), a course of several months that local churches offer.

Why are infants baptized? How can an infant or young child really believe in Jesus and his teaching?

We have said that sacraments require faith, and normally the one receiving the sacrament expresses that faith personally. Baptism, however, is unique in that it is the normal way that Jesus saves a person from sin and death and gives him or her spiritual life. The Holy Spirit comes to live in the person through this sacrament.

In New Testament times most people entering the Church were adults, although in a few places the Bible mentions that so-and-so was baptized "and his whole household" (Acts 10:48; 16:15, 31–33; 18:8; 1 Corinthians 1:16), which may have included children. When Jesus' apostles wanted to prevent little children from coming to him for a blessing, Jesus "was indignant" and said, "Let the children come to me, do not hinder them; for to such belongs the kingdom of God" (Mark 10:13–16).

If the kingdom of God belongs to little children, how could the Church refuse to offer children and infants the saving grace of Jesus through baptism? Saint Paul compared baptism with circumcision, which was normally administered to children (see Colossians 2:11–12). The Church is not for adults only. It is God's family, God's people, and a family includes the youngest to the oldest.

Baptism does require faith, and the parents and godparents accept baptism for the child in faith, committing themselves to pass on that faith to the child through the years. It is interesting that when some parents approached Jesus to ask him to expel a demon from a child (see Mark 9:17–27) or even to raise a child from the dead (Mark 5:22–23, 35–43), Jesus did these works in response to the *parents'* faith, not the child's. There is a parallel here.

When children grow up, however, they must each make their own personal choice whether or not to follow Jesus and live as a Christian. They must affirm their baptism. Each year the Catholic Church stresses the importance of this personal decision and commitment to the Lord by calling upon each person to renew the baptismal covenant or promises at the Easter liturgy.

Finally, baptizing an infant or young child is another reminder that the grace of salvation through baptism is a free gift of God, not something that a person deserves or earns. It is very clear when an infant is baptized that salvation is *God's* work. Just as a child does not personally choose to be born, parents can cooperate with God's plan by bringing their children to the font of baptism to be reborn in Christ. What more marvelous gift, in addition to natural human life, can a parent choose to give?

Is it ever necessary for a person to be baptized a second time? For example, what if someone who is baptized leaves the Church, rejects Jesus or stops believing in God and then the person repents?

No one who is validly baptized can be baptized again ("rebaptized"), even if he or she rejected God and fell away from the faith for a time. Baptism is permanent.

Physically we are born only once, and baptism is a new birth. Jesus told Nicodemus that we must be "born anew" or "born of water and the Spirit" (John 3:3–6). Through this sacrament a person is born anew with God's life (called "sanctifying grace") and born into a new family—the Church.

Like the prodigal son (see Luke 15:11–32), once you are part of God's family through baptism, you are always a member: You are a son or daughter of God, not an outsider. All one needs to do to come home to life in the Church is to come to Jesus in the sacrament of reconciliation or penance, receive God's mercy and forgiveness and begin to live again in the freedom of a son or daughter of God, the freedom received in baptism.

What is the Eucharist? Why do Catholics believe that it is really the Body, Blood, soul and divinity of Jesus Christ?

Sometimes Catholics have been accused of not taking the Bible literally enough. The important thing is to understand what the Bible really means to teach. In the case of the Eucharist, the Catholic Church believes that Jesus' teaching is unmistakably clear, even though it seems impossible. ("With God, nothing will be impossible," Luke 1:37.)

In instituting the Eucharist at the Last Supper, Jesus took the Passover bread and said, "Take, eat; this is my body" (Matthew 26:26). Then taking the cup of blessing, he said, "This is my blood of the covenant, which is poured out for many for the forgiveness of sins" (Matthew 26:28).

Some Christians say that Jesus meant this bread to represent or "symbolize" his body. After all, "How can this man give us his flesh to eat?" (John 6:52). Yes, this is the question that people posed to Jesus in the Gospel of Saint John. But what was Jesus' response?

> Truly, truly, I say to you, unless you eat the flesh of the Son of man and drink his blood, you have no life in you; he who eats my flesh and drinks my blood has eternal life, and I will raise him up at the last day. For my flesh is food indeed, and my blood is drink indeed. He who eats

my flesh and drinks my blood abides in me, and I in him.
(John 6:53–56)

Some people will argue that the Gospel of John is symbolic.
For example, Jesus says, "I am the door [or gate] of the
sheep.... I am the door; if any one enters by me, he will be
saved" (John 10:7, 9). Jesus is the "door" to heaven, but he
doesn't have a handle and is not made of wood. In the same
Gospel, Jesus says that you must eat his flesh and drink
his blood to be saved, even when "many of his disciples
drew back and no longer walked with him" (John 6:66). It
seems that Jesus meant what he said: that his followers
must eat his flesh and drink his blood to be saved.

Jesus did not back down or soften his teaching. Rather
he turned to the twelve apostles and said, "Will you also go
away?" Thankfully, Peter, the head of the twelve, replied
on behalf of them all, "Lord, to whom shall we go? You have
the words of eternal life; and we have believed, and have
come to know, that you are the Holy One of God" (John
6:67–69).

For two thousand years the Catholic Church has pro-
fessed its belief in the real presence of Jesus: that is, "the
body and blood, together with the soul and divinity, of our
Lord Jesus Christ...*is truly, really, and substantially* contained [Council of Trent (1551): DS 1651]" in the Eucharist
(*CCC*, 1374, quoting the Council of Trent).

What does "the real presence" mean? The Eucharist appears to be bread and wine. How can it be Jesus?

Jesus was truly human; it takes faith to see beyond his
humanity and to accept the fact that he is a divine Person,

the Son of God, who was, is and always will be with God the Father and the Holy Spirit.

In the same way, the Eucharist appears outwardly to be bread and wine. It takes faith in the words of Jesus to accept the fact that the bread and wine become Jesus' Body and Blood when the priest pronounces Jesus' words, "This is my body.... This is my blood," as Jesus commanded, "Do this in remembrance of me" (see Luke 22:19). While the outward appearance continues to be that of bread and wine, what we can't see, taste or feel is the divinity of Jesus Christ fully and really present. The essential transformation of the elements into the Body and Blood of Jesus is called *transubstantiation*.

As the Godhead was hidden in Jesus while he walked the earth, so the Godhead is hidden in the Eucharist. In both cases we can see God's great love and humility. What an amazing thing that the eternal, almighty God would take the form, first, of our humanity and then, humbler yet, of physical food to nourish us in his Spirit.

Why do Catholics have to attend Mass every Sunday?

If you heard that God was going to make a personal appearance, bringing special grace, healing and blessing, would you show up?

Given the risk that someone will say no, let me explain that God formed the Church to be a people who know, love and serve him. The most important event in human history is when Jesus, the Son of God, rose from the dead on Easter Sunday. On that day Satan and sin were conquered forever. Not only was the human race restored to friendship with God, but also all who accept this gift of salvation are destined to live forever with God in the glory of heaven. This is certainly something to celebrate!

What return can God's people make for what God has done for us in Jesus Christ? We come together once a week, as a people, on Sunday—the Lord's Day, the day of Jesus' resurrection—to worship God and offer thanksgiving. (*Eucharist* means "thanksgiving"!) Christians have done this weekly since the Church was born on Pentecost. The center of this worship, called the Mass, is the reading and proclamation of the sacred Scripture, always including a reading from one of the four Gospels, and reception of the Eucharist, the Body and Blood of Jesus Christ.

A Catholic who asks, "Why do I have to go to Mass on Sunday?" is like a football player who asks, "Why do I have to show up for the game on Friday night?" "Showing up" is what the thing is all about! If you don't want to play football when the team plays, why be a football player? If you don't want to worship God when the Church gathers, then why be a Catholic?

The Mass, according to the Sacred Vatican Council,

> is the summit toward which the activity of the Church is directed; it is also the fount from which all her power flows. For the goal of apostolic endeavor is that all who are made sons [and daughters] of God by faith and baptism should come together to praise God in the midst of his Church, to take part in the sacrifice and to eat the Lord's Supper. (Constitution on the Sacred Liturgy, 10)

Catholics call the Mass a sacrifice. Wasn't Jesus only sacrificed once, on Calvary? Why do Catholics "re-sacrifice" Christ?

First, the Mass is not only a sacrifice but, the Second Vatican Council says, "a sacrament of love, a sign of unity, a bond of charity, a paschal banquet in which Christ is consumed, the mind is filled with grace, and a pledge of future glory is given to us" (Constitution on the Sacred Liturgy, 47).

Second, Catholics know that Christ "entered once for all into the Holy Place, taking not the blood of goats and calves but his own blood, thus securing an eternal redemption" (Hebrews 9:12; see also 7:27; 9:28). Jesus' *physical* sacrifice took place only once, on Calvary. But Jesus also directed his apostles to meet together to speak the words, "This is my body.... This is my blood," in his memory. In the Mass Jesus' real Body and real Blood are made present and shared, and this continues and will continue until the end of time. Jesus' *one* sacrifice on Calvary is made present, or perpetuated, in the Mass.

Vatican II once again explains simply and beautifully:

At the Last Supper, on the night he was betrayed, our Savior instituted the eucharistic sacrifice of his Body and Blood. This he did in order to perpetuate the sacrifice of the Cross throughout the ages until he should come again, and so to entrust to his beloved Spouse, the Church, a memorial of his death and resurrection. (Constitution on the Sacred Liturgy, 47)

Why can't Catholics receive communion in other churches, and why can't other Christians receive Jesus at a Catholic liturgy?

Celebrating the Eucharist and receiving Communion express the deep unity we have as Catholics who have received the same faith and are in full unity or communion with all other Catholics, including the pope and the bishops in union with him, throughout the world. Thus for Catholics, receiving Communion at Mass is not just a private act of faith in Jesus but also a public proclamation or witness of our unity with all those who share the same faith and are shepherded by the same pastors—Catholic priests, bishops and the pope.

The closest analogy we have is the sacrament of marriage, in which a married person only expresses the fullness of love with his or her spouse, the person with whom he or she has made the marriage covenant. Catholics normally only receive the Eucharist in a Catholic Church because we are only fully united or covenanted with Catholics. Thus, Catholics see the Eucharist as a *sign* of unity that already exists. Of course, receiving the Eucharist together also deepens and strengthens the unity that already is present among Catholics.

One difference from the marriage analogy is that in special circumstances a Catholic could receive the Eucharist in an Orthodox Church, because the Orthodox have a valid priesthood and also believe that the Eucharist is truly the Body and Blood of Jesus. If a Catholic does not have access to the Eucharist for an extended period of time in a Catholic church or mission, he or she can seek permission from the bishop to receive the Eucharist in an Orthodox church. It also is possible in special circumstances for an Orthodox Christian to receive the Eucharist from a minister of the Catholic Church.

What is the sacrament of reconciliation?

Forgiveness is at the heart of the message of Jesus. The Old Testament tried to limit retribution—"eye for eye, tooth for tooth" (Exodus 21:24)—but Jesus taught his followers to love their enemies, pray for their persecutors and forgive others without limit (see Matthew 5:38; 43–44;

18:21–22). The really good news is that Jesus teaches this because he knew that God loves and forgives each of us without limit.

Jesus shocked the Jewish leaders when he told a paralyzed man that his sins were forgiven. The response was: "It is blasphemy! Who can forgive sins but God alone?" (Mark 2:7). That's the point! Jesus possessed the authority to forgive sins.

Jesus gave this same authority to his apostles: "As the Father has sent me, even so I send you.... Receive the Holy Spirit. If you forgive the sins of any, they are forgiven; if you retain the sins of any, they are retained" (John 20:21–23). Thus Jesus established forgiveness and reconciliation as a sacrament, mediated through the authority of those who lead the Church. The sacrament of penance is a sure means of God's grace and mercy.

Didn't Jesus say we should forgive each other? Why do we have to go to a priest for forgiveness of sins? Why not go directly to God?

Yes, Jesus commanded all of his followers to forgive when someone sinned against them (see Matthew 6:14; Matthew 18:21–22; Luke 17:3–4). But Jesus also gave his apostles a special authority to "bind and loose" or to forgive sins in God's name.

Many people wonder whether God has forgiven or can forgive them, even when other people have forgiven them and tell them that God forgives them. Sound psychology points out the wonderful healing, even therapeutic, power of the sacrament of reconciliation. A priest, who represents both Christ and the Christian community, absolves a person—that is, declares him or her free from sin in Jesus' name—based on his word to the apostles, "If you forgive the sins of any, they are forgiven" (John 20:23).

Of course, we can and should go directly to God in a prayer of sorrow and repentance whenever we sin. Whenever we pray the Lord's Prayer, we ask God the Father to forgive us as we forgive others. But in the incarnational and sacramental way that God has come to us in Jesus, the sacrament of reconciliation makes this prayer a living encounter with God's mercy through a person who represents Jesus and his Church. Once again, as with all the sacraments, Jesus comes to us in the sacrament of reconciliation personally and in the flesh to declare that our sins are forgiven. This confirms that he is truly Emmanuel, "God with us."

Why is confirmation a sacrament? Don't we receive the Holy Spirit in baptism? Don't many people receive a new outpouring of the Holy Spirit without this sacrament?

Jesus established the sacraments as sure ways that God's grace comes to us and that God acts in our lives, but God is not limited to acting through the sacraments. So the Holy Spirit, like "the wind [which] blows where it wills" (John 3:8), can and does come to people in many ways.

The sacrament of confirmation is the means by which the Church formally asks the Father to send the Holy Spirit, as Jesus commanded, and trusts in Jesus' words: "How much more will the heavenly Father give the Holy Spirit to those who ask him!" (Luke 11:13). In confirmation the Christian becomes more clearly an image of Jesus, upon whom the Holy Spirit rested. This we see in Jesus' baptism in the Jordan River (see Matthew 3:16–17; Mark 1:9–11; Luke 3:21–22).

As the prophet Isaiah said of the Messiah, the anointed one of God:

> There shall come forth a shoot from the stump of Jesse [King David's father],
>   and a branch shall grow out of his roots.
> And the Spirit of the LORD shall rest upon him,
>   the spirit of wisdom and understanding,
>   the spirit of counsel and might,
>   the spirit of knowledge and the fear of the LORD.
> And his delight shall be in the fear of the LORD [piety].
> (Isaiah 11:1–3)

Those seven gifts of the Holy Spirit—wisdom, understanding, counsel, fortitude (might), knowledge, fear of the Lord and piety—are gifts that came in fullness to the Messiah, Jesus, and that come to all Christians through the special sacrament of the Holy Spirit, confirmation.

Again, by recognizing confirmation as a sacrament, the Church declares that Jesus fulfills his promise to send the Spirit to his followers (see Luke 24:49; Acts 1:8; 2; 16–17) whenever the sacrament is celebrated. In the Catholic Church the bishop is normally the one who confers this sacrament, because he represents Jesus and the apostles in a special way.

What is the sacrament of the anointing of the sick?

The scriptural roots of the sacrament of the anointing the sick are very clear: Jesus healed the sick and commanded and empowered his disciples to do the same. "And they cast out many demons, and anointed with oil many that were sick and healed them" (Mark 6:13).

The ordained leaders of the early Church continued this practice:

> Is any among you sick? Let him call for the elders of the
> Church, and let them pray over him, anointing him with
> oil in the name of the Lord; and the prayer of faith
> will save the sick man, and the Lord will raise him
> up; and if he has committed sins, he will be forgiven.
> (James 5:14–15)

The Church has administered this sacrament since its earliest days, but its focus has shifted at times. Until recently the emphasis was on preparation for death, but the Second Vatican Council restored an emphasis on prayer for physical and spiritual healing for all seriously ill persons (see Constitution on the Sacred Liturgy, 73; Decree on the Ministry and Life of Priests, 5).

Can't we all pray for the sick? Why do we need a special sacrament for this?

As we have seen, sacraments are not the only ways that God works. Of course anyone can and should pray for the healing and blessing of God for a sick person. Usually when an illness is prolonged or serious, a Catholic also can call upon the healing power of Jesus through this sacrament.

This sacrament exists in response to Jesus' healing ministry and to the fact that Jesus gave those who represented him, the apostles, a particular grace and power to heal (see Acts 3:1–10; 5:12–16; 8:4–8; 14:8–10; 28:8). Healing is a special part of the ministry of the Church.

Do Catholics believe that everyone who receives the sacrament of the anointing of the sick (or any healing prayer) will be healed?

The sacrament does not guarantee that every sick person will be healed physically. God's ways are above our ways, and often he will allow sickness or suffering to continue. Many texts in the New Testament exhort Christians to rejoice in their sufferings and to consider them a sharing in the suffering of Christ (see Romans 8:16–17; 2 Corinthians 4:16–18; Colossians 1:24; 2 Timothy 2:11–12; 1 Peter 4:13). Sometimes when Christians pray for healing, God works on a deeper level than the physical—imparting peace and strength, inspiring virtue and drawing the person into a closer relationship with him.

Yet our God is a healing God, and he often works through the sacrament of the anointing of the sick to restore physical health. Catholics will see the power of God manifest as they pray for the sick with expectant faith and call upon his healing power through this sacrament.

What is the sacrament of holy orders?

From among his many followers, Jesus set apart certain men—especially "the twelve"—to bear a unique responsibility to carry on his mission and ministry. To prepare them for this, Jesus gave them special formation. He then gave them the authority to forgive sins, to preside over the breaking of the bread—the Eucharist—in his memory and to instruct and guide new disciples.

The apostles and the leaders they appointed passed on their authority and ministry to others in a particular way. In the New Testament the apostles were set apart for ministry by the prayer, fasting and "laying on of hands" of the Christian community. In the Acts of the Apostles, for example, the first deacons were ordained in this way:

> And they chose Stephen, a man full of faith and of the Holy Spirit, and Philip, and Prochorus, and Nicanor, and Timon, and Parmenas, and Nicolaus, a proselyte of

Antioch. These they set before the apostles, and they prayed and laid their hands upon them. (Acts 6:5–6)

In Acts 13, "while they were worshiping the Lord and fasting, the Holy Spirit said, 'Set apart for me Barnabas and Saul for the work to which I have called them.' Then after fasting and praying they laid their hands on them and sent them off" (Acts 13:2–3). These biblical accounts show us the origin of the sacrament of holy orders in the early Church.

Why do Catholics require priests to be celibate—abstaining from all sexual activity?

Celibacy is a requirement of the priesthood that Roman Catholics teach and respect because of the biblical evidence for its value and its successful practice over many centuries. The Bible testifies to the fact that Jesus valued celibacy. Jesus himself was celibate, and he taught his disciples about this way of life: "Not all men can receive this precept, but only those to whom it is given. For there are eunuchs who have been so from birth, and...there are eunuchs who have made themselves eunuchs for the sake of the kingdom of heaven. He who is able to receive this, let him receive it" (Matthew 19:11–12).

Likewise, Saint Paul instructed:

> I wish that all were as I myself am. But each has his own special gift from God, one of one kind and one of another....
>
> I want you to be free from anxieties. The unmarried man is anxious about the affairs of the Lord, how to please the Lord; but the married man is anxious about worldly affairs, how to please his wife, and his interests are divided.... I say this for your own benefit, not to lay

> any restraint upon you, but to promote good order and to secure your undivided devotion to the Lord. (1 Corinthians 7:7, 32–34a, 35)

Jesus and Paul both make it clear that celibacy is not a call given to everyone but rather a gift that enables a person to devote his or her undivided attention to the affairs of the Lord and his kingdom. Since the days of the early Church, men and women have committed themselves to God in this way, and so it should not be surprising that by the tenth century the Catholic Church of the Latin rite confirmed the single state of life as a requirement for the priesthood. The primary thought behind this is the imitation of Jesus.

Celibacy is also a sign or a witness to the world. It involves renouncing some undeniably good things—sexual pleasure within marriage and the good of married life—for another good: greater freedom to devote time and attention to the Lord and to the building up of his body, the Church.

Celibacy, however, is not an *absolute* requirement for priesthood. Some married male Protestant ministers who become Catholic are given special permission to be ordained in the Catholic Church as married men, since they already are married. The Eastern rites of the Catholic Church allow married men to be ordained to the priesthood. This practice reflects their culture and Christian tradition, just as celibacy reflects the call of God to the Western branch of the Catholic Church, Roman Catholicism.

Why do Catholics call priests "Father" when Jesus said, "Call no man your father on earth, for you have one Father, who is in heaven" (Matthew 23:9)?

The Catholic understanding of Jesus' teaching is that no human being may be given the honor and respect due only to God the Father. The apostle Paul called himself a father to the Corinthians: "For though you have countless guides in Christ, you do not have many fathers. For I became your father in Christ Jesus through the gospel" (1 Corinthians 4:15; see also 1 Thessalonians 2:9–12). It is in this sense that Catholics apply the title "Father" to priests.

Why are there so many titles for ordained ministers of the Catholic Church? I find it confusing when Catholics talk about priests, bishops, archbishops, abbots and so on.

The various titles of ordained ministers in the Catholic Church—priest, bishop, archbishop, abbot, cardinal and so on—distinguish the different roles or offices of these ministers. For example, an archbishop is simply the bishop of a large, prominent diocese, sometimes an ancient one, with many people under his care. An abbot is the head of a community of monks; the name is taken from *abba,* meaning "father"—in this case the spiritual father of the monks.

In the Catholic understanding, the bishops—a category that includes the pope, archbishops and most cardinals—possess "the fullness of the sacrament of [Holy] Orders" (Dogmatic Constitution on the Church, 21), while priests and deacons share in and extend the priestly ministry of their bishop. This understanding is based on the way ordained leadership actually evolved and functioned in the early centuries of Christianity, which Catholics believe the Holy Spirit of God directed.

The Catholic Church decided in the eleventh century to have a special group of ministers, the college of cardinals, to elect the pope. This was necessary because some secular rulers (kings and emperors) had claimed the right to choose the pope and to confer on him authority to rule the Church. The college of cardinals put the election of the pope back into the Church, where it rightfully belongs.

The important thing about these offices is that they all share in the ministry of Jesus Christ. These ordained ministers are all set apart for leadership and service in the body of Christ.

What spiritual qualities does a man need in order to be a priest?

A priest must be a man of prayer, must witness to Christ and his gospel by his life and must possess the gifts (charisms) to be a servant-leader of the Christian community. Through the sacrament of holy orders, God and the Christian community set the priest apart to fulfill a special role in the body of Christ. The model for that role is Jesus himself, who laid down his life for his sheep.

Why does a priest need a special sacrament, the sacrament of holy orders, to serve and lead the Church?

Besides a deep relationship with the Lord and personal qualities that make him suitable for priesthood, the priest must be empowered by God, just as Jesus' first apostles were, to carry out the mission that Jesus performed: to proclaim the Good News of the kingdom, teach with authority, forgive sins, pray with others for healing and deliverance from evil spirits. A phrase from Acts 6 sums up the core of this ministry: "prayer and ministry of the word." The sacrament of holy orders sets a man apart for priestly ministry and empowers him to carry it out by the grace of God.

The priest, through his ordination, also receives the authority that Jesus gave to the twelve at the Last Supper to offer the bread and wine of the Eucharist to the Father in Jesus' name. Jesus told the twelve to "do this in remembrance of me" (Luke 22:19). The priest should expect the power of God to be available to him, for Jesus told his disciples that if they had faith in him, they would do even greater works than he did (see John 14:12).

Jesus never spoke directly about marriage as a sacrament. Why do Catholics consider it a sacrament?

Catholics believe that Jesus raised marriage to a new level. Of course, Jesus recognized that the roots of marriage go back to the beginning of creation. He quoted the book of Genesis, the first book of the Bible:

> Have you not read that he who made them from the beginning made them male and female, and said, "For this reason a man shall leave his father and mother and be joined to his wife, and the two shall become one"? So they are no longer two but one. What therefore God has joined together, let no man put asunder." (Matthew 19:4–6)

Why is marriage a sacrament? First, because it is an action of God: "What...God has joined together, let no man put asunder." Jesus was adamant about this, and he reestablished the indissolubility of marriage that existed before the Fall: "For your hardness of heart Moses allowed you to divorce your wives, but from the beginning it was not so. And I say to you: whoever divorces his wife, except for unchastity, and marries another, commits adultery" (Matthew 19:8–9).

Marriage is a sacrament because Jesus invested it with the grace and power that existed "in the beginning," when God directly gave this grace of fidelity to Adam and Eve before their sin. Now it is only through God's power, conferred in this sacrament, that two human beings are able to faithfully live out this high calling to become one flesh.

Since Jesus confers the grace that enables a Christian couple to be faithful for life, he consequently expects and demands that we live according to the grace and power he provides. The Jewish people before Jesus' coming may have tolerated divorce, but now it is forbidden because of the grace of Jesus Christ, available through this sacrament. (There are instances when a marriage can be annulled. In these cases the Church judges that the conditions of a true marriage did not exist.)

Marriage is also a sacrament because it is a visible, outward sign of Jesus' presence and love in the world. The love of a husband for his wife, for example, is a sign of Christ's love for the Church:

> Husbands, love your wives, as Christ loved the Church and gave himself up for her, that he might sanctify her.... For no man ever hates his own flesh, but nourishes it and cherishes it, as Christ does the Church, because we are members of his body.... This is a great mystery, and I mean in reference to Christ and the Church. (Ephesians 5:25–26, 29–30, 32)

God gives the husband the call and power to love his wife as Christ loved the Church—even to the point of death. Likewise he calls wives to love and submit to their husbands as the Church loves and submits to Christ. Were marriage not a sacrament with special graces, this too would be impossible.

Chapter Eight

The Saints: Our Friends in Glory

Saint John wrote, "That which we have seen and heard we proclaim also to you, so that you may have fellowship with us; and our fellowship is with the Father and with his Son Jesus Christ" (1 John 1:3). Saint John has died. Do we here on earth still have fellowship with him in the Father and in his Son Jesus Christ? Are we in communion with him, more than just as a memory, but as a living relationship between people who are alive in Jesus Christ?

The Catholic Church says yes. We believe that the fellowship that we have with the faithful followers of Jesus on earth continues even after death. This we call "the communion of saints."

How does the Bible describe those who have died but are united to God—part of this "communion of saints"?

The Letter to the Hebrews says, "We are surrounded by so great a cloud of witnesses" (Hebrews 12:1), referring to the saints who have gone before us. The book of Revelation (to John) refers to 144,000 (the "perfect number": twelve times twelve times a thousand) who "have been redeemed from mankind as first fruits for God and the Lamb [Jesus]" and who "sing a new song before the throne [of God]" (Revelation 14:3).

Is there communication between the saints who have died and those still on earth?

We must make some important distinctions in answering this question. Catholics believe that there is communication through prayer between those on earth and those who have died in God's grace. This communication is based on the *communion* or fellowship in Jesus Christ that exists between the saints (literally, "holy ones," those who belong to God) on earth and those in heaven. The Catholic Church, in fact, calls this "the communion of saints," and we profess belief in this in some of the earliest Christian creeds, like the Apostles' Creed: "I believe in the communion of saints, the forgiveness of sins, the resurrection of the body and life everlasting."

On the other hand, there are many false and dangerous ways in which people attempt to communicate with the dead outside of Christ. These the Catholic Church refers to as spiritism or occult practices. The Church condemns them as sins against the first commandment: "I am the LORD your God.... You shall have no other gods before me" (Exodus 20:2, 3).

The *Catechism of the Catholic Church* lists specific occult practices that are forbidden because they try to control the spirit world or contact people or spiritual forces apart from Jesus Christ. Therefore these practices lie outside of God's will:

> All forms of *divination* are to be rejected: recourse to Satan or demons, conjuring up the dead or other practices falsely supposed to "unveil" the future [Cf. *Deut*

18:10; *Jer* 29:8]. Consulting horoscopes, astrology, palm reading, interpretation of omens and lots, the phenomena of clairvoyance, and recourse to mediums all conceal a desire for power over time, history, and, in the last analysis, other human beings, as well as a wish to conciliate hidden powers. They contradict the honor, respect, and loving fear that we owe to God alone.

All practices of *magic* or *sorcery,* by which one attempts to tame occult powers, so as to place them at one's service and have a supernatural power over others—even if this were for the sake of restoring their health—are gravely contrary to the virtue of religion. These practices are even more to be condemned when accompanied by the intention of harming someone, or when they have recourse to the intervention of demons. Wearing charms is also reprehensible. *Spiritism* often implies divination or magical practices; the Church for her part warns the faithful against it. Recourse to so-called traditional cures does not justify either the invocation of evil powers or the exploitation of another's credulity. (*CCC*, 2116–2117)

How can people on earth be in communion or contact with the saints in heaven?

Saint Paul wrote letters in which he called his fellow Christians "saints" or "holy ones" (see Romans 12:13; 16:15; 1 Corinthians 16:1, 15; 2 Corinthians 1:1; Ephesians 1:1; Philippians1:1; 4:21–22; Philemon 5). For Catholics, then, the communion of saints includes *all* of God's people—those in heaven, those on earth and even those who have died still in need of being cleansed and purified of some sin (Catholics call these the souls in *purgatory*). All of these people are in a real relationship with God through

Jesus Christ. They are "one body in Christ, and individually members one of another" (Romans 12:5).

Catholics traditionally have called the saints still on earth the *church militant,* who still "fight the good fight of the faith" (1 Timothy 6:12); those in purgatory the *church suffering* from the pain of purification from sin; and those in heaven the *church triumphant.* (Note that there are not three separate churches but one Church of Jesus Christ transcending space and time.)

Can the saints in heaven help those on earth?

The saints in heaven are a great support for us on earth, especially if we realize the help that the saints can give and ask them for it. Unfortunately, many Christians don't realize this. In his book *The Screwtape Letters,* the twentieth-century Christian writer C.S. Lewis tells of an imaginary discussion between a junior demon and his mentor, a crafty devil named Screwtape. Screwtape tells the young demon that one of the greatest "allies" of their evil is the ignorance of the Church on earth about the saints in heaven, who are "spread out through all time and space and rooted in eternity, terrible as an army with banners. That, I confess, is a spectacle which makes our boldest tempters uneasy. But fortunately it is quite invisible to these humans."[1]

The fact is that very few people even think that the human race is in the middle of a battle, the battle between God, with his angels and saints, and Satan, with his demons and those on earth who have chosen to do evil. Do you realize that you are in the midst of a spiritual battle? The Letter to the Ephesians says:

> Be strong in the Lord and in the strength of his might.
> Put on the whole armor of God, that you may be able to
> stand against the wiles of the devil. For we are not con-
> tending against flesh and blood, but against the princi-
> palities, against the powers, against the world rulers of
> this present darkness, against the spiritual hosts of
> wickedness in the heavenly places. (Ephesians 6:10–12)

But before we get carried away with images of battle,
remember that the battle is about having the courage to
make good and right choices every day. For this we need to
"be strong in the Lord and in the strength of his might."
And the saints in heaven can help, because they have
shown that strength in their lives.

This is the first way the saints help us, by their example. Read the lives of the saints the Catholic Church has
canonized. There is something in the life of each saint to
inspire and encourage us. Each saint exhibits a particular
form of strength in his or her decisions and actions, and by
this each one frustrates and defeats the devil and advances
God's plan and his kingdom. "Therefore, since we are surrounded by so great a cloud of witnesses, let us...run with
perseverance the race that is set before us" (Hebrews 12:1).

Besides inspiring us by their example, the saints in
heaven also help us by their *prayers* or *intercession*. This
raises the following question.

Why do Catholics pray to the saints and ask them to pray to God on our behalf?

Most of us have asked another Christian—another "saint"
in the body of Christ—to pray for us when we have had a
particular need. The apostle Paul frequently asked other
disciples of Jesus to pray for him (see Romans 15:30–32;

Ephesians 6:18–19; Colossians 4:3; 1 Thessalonians 5:25; 2 Thessalonians 3:1). Other New Testament writers also urge us to pray for each other for healing or deliverance from sin (James 5:13–18; 1 John 5:16). Prayer seems to be a normal way for the saints on earth to support each other.

Catholics believe that we also can ask for prayers from the saints who already are united with the Lord. If the prayers of certain Christians here on earth seem to have special power because of their great faith or holiness, how much more powerful and effective are the prayers of those who are united to God in heaven!

What does the Bible say about this? John speaks about the saints in heaven, the "twenty-four elders" gathered around God's throne, offering to God "golden bowls full of incense, which are the prayers of the saints" (Revelation 5:8). Here we have a beautiful image of intercession: The saints in heaven offer the prayers of those on earth to the heavenly Father. This is exactly what the saints do for us.

Christians do not worship the saints. Christians petition the saints to pray for us or to offer our prayers to God the Father, always in the name of Jesus and in the power of the Holy Spirit.

When a teacher in the fourth century questioned this practice, Saint Jerome replied:

> You say in your book that while we live we are able to pray for each other, but afterwards when we have died, the prayer of no person for another can be heard.... But if the Apostles and martyrs while still in the body can pray for others, at a time when they ought still to be solicitous about themselves, how much more will they do so after their crowns, victories, and triumphs?[2]

How does the Church on earth know who is in heaven, who are the saints?

The Catholic Church believes that God attests to the holiness of a saint by the holiness of his or her life here on earth and by signs or miracles worked through prayers offered in the saint's name after death.

Canonization is the name for the Church's process of examining the life of someone to see if he or she should be declared a saint. The road to canonization begins with the Church declaring a person as a "Servant of God."

If the person is found to have lived a life of heroic virtue, he or she is declared "Venerable." A verified miracle (usually a physical healing) occurring through the person's intercession may lead to beatification, in which the person is venerated as "Blessed." When a second miracle through the person's intercession is verified, then the person is canonized—declared to be a saint—and can be venerated by the whole Church. The Church does not require any miracles in the case of a martyr.

Canonized saints represent only a few of those who are actually in glory with the Lord. The Church does not hold up canonized saints as members of an exclusive club but as examples and models of holiness, representing all of the saints in heaven.

The diversity of the saints assures that there is a model for every Christian. The canonized include people from every state or situation of life: men and women, married and celibate, active and contemplative, young and old, rich and poor, kings and ordinary people. Some led public lives and interacted with thousands of people; others were little known during their lives, but later reports about their lives or about miracles worked through their intercession attested to their holiness.

Doesn't this focus on the saints take away from the worship due to Jesus alone? Isn't it idolatry to pray to the saints instead of to God?

In the Old Testament God calls himself a "jealous" God (Exodus 20:5). However, this means, "You shall worship no other god" (Exodus 34:14). The saints are not God, and Christians are not to worship them.

To have a proper relationship with the saints, one should approach them as members of that great family, the Church, that Jesus founded. As Saint Paul said, "We, though many, are one body in Christ, and individually members one of another" (Romans 12:5). All who belong to Jesus Christ are united in him in the Church, with God as our Father. Christians have real unity and fellowship with those who have run the race of the Christian life on earth and have attained the glory of heaven.

We address the saints, whom we cannot see, just as Jesus spoke with Moses and Elijah in the presence of Peter, James and John on Mount Tabor at his transfiguration (see Matthew 17:1–5). This event revealed the glory of Jesus' divinity. The saints have attained the glory of heaven and are radiant with the splendor of God, just as Moses and Elijah reflected on Mount Tabor the light and glory that they received from God through Jesus. For this we honor the saints in heaven.

We join the saints in the eternal chorus of praise to God our Savior.

> And the twenty-four elders and the four living creatures fell down and worshiped God who is seated on the

throne, saying, "Amen. Hallelujah!...

Praise our God, all you his servants,

you who fear him, small and great." (Revelation 19:4, 5)

We also can ask the saints for their prayers, just as we ask those on earth who know and love Christ to pray for us. This comes naturally to those who know how families relate. God the Father's jealousy is not the type that would preclude his children's speaking to each other and supporting each other.

The Catholic Church knows that the saints in heaven are not just enjoying God for themselves. God is love, and he longs for the salvation of all people here on earth. The saints share in the love and charity of God toward us on earth. Saint Thérèse of Lisieux, a young Carmelite sister who lived in the nineteenth century and died at the age of twenty-four, said that she wanted to spend her heaven doing good on earth.[3]

Why do Christians imitate the saints? Isn't Jesus our only model?

Of course, Jesus Christ is the ultimate model for all Christians, and those who have followed him throughout the ages reflect his glory in the various circumstances of their lives. God calls all of us to reflect Jesus Christ; Saint Paul told the Galatians that he was in travail "until Christ be formed in you!" (Galatians 4:19). Yet Paul boldly said of himself, "Be imitators of me, as I am of Christ" (1 Corinthians 11:1), and, "Take as your guide those who follow the example that we set" (see Philippians 3:17).

We know that people set an example for others by their way of life, either good or bad. Saints are great role models because they imitate and reflect Jesus in different vocations, times and circumstances. A truly Christlike person reminds us of Jesus and leads us to Jesus. The canonized saints of the Catholic Church are people in history who clearly reflect Jesus Christ and lead people to him by their lives, their words and their teachings.

The Second Vatican Council had a powerful statement of this:

> For when we look at the lives of those who have faithfully followed Christ, we are inspired with a new reason for seeking the city which is to come (Heb. 13:14; 11:10). At the same time we are shown a most safe path by which...we will be able to arrive at perfect union with Christ, that is, holiness. In the lives of those who shared in our humanity and yet were transformed into especially successful images of Christ (cf. 2 Cor. 3:18), God vividly manifests to men His presence and His face. He speaks to us in them, and gives us a sign of His kingdom, to which we are powerfully drawn, surrounded as we are by so many witnesses (cf. Heb. 12:1), and having such an argument for the truth of the gospel. (Dogmatic Constitution on the Church, 50)[4]

Why do Catholics keep pictures, statues and even relics of the saints? Isn't this superstitious?

If you go into any home, you probably see pictures or other mementos of members of the family who live there, even of those who have died. These mementos are family treasures; they keep family memories alive.

The saints are members of our great family, the Church, and so we may have images or relics of them to remind us of their presence. These mementos also remind us that we belong to a family, the Church, and that we wish to stay connected with this family. The pictures or statues might remind us of that saint's virtues, of how the saint followed and reflected Jesus, or they might remind us to ask them to pray for us.

A relic is a part of a saint's body or something the saint touched during life—perhaps a piece of clothing or a rosary. Such items have no magic power of their own, but healings and other miracles have been reported when people have come into contact with relics and prayed and believed in Jesus and his healing power. This should not surprise a Christian. After all, when people who had faith in Jesus touched his garments, they were healed (see Mark 5:25–34). The Acts of the Apostles reports that some people were healed or freed from demons when handkerchiefs that had touched the body of Saint Paul were used in prayer (Acts 19:11–12). Even Saint Peter's shadow is reported to have brought healing (Acts 5:15).

There is always the danger that people will begin to think that the statue or the relic itself has magical power. We can avoid superstition or abuse if we remember that any power to convert hearts, to deliver from evil or to heal comes only from God through Jesus Christ and the power of the Holy Spirit.

In short, pictures, statues, relics and the like are physical reminders that can stir up our faith in God and remind us of God's presence and goodness. God also may use them occasionally as instruments of his saving and healing love.

Are some saints in heaven greater than others? Do we know who is the greatest saint?

Jesus simply said that many of the last on earth would be the first in the kingdom of heaven (see Mark 10:31), and that "whoever humbles himself like this child, he is the greatest in the kingdom of heaven" (Matthew 18:4). He corrected his disciples when they argued over who would get the best seats in God's kingdom, telling them,

> Whoever would be great among you must be your servant, and whoever would be first among you must be slave of all. For the Son of man also came not to be served but to serve, and to give his life as a ransom for many. (Mark 10:43–45)

As to the greatest saint, Jesus praised John the Baptist but with a rather puzzling conclusion: "Truly, I say to you, among those born of women there has arisen no one greater than John the Baptist; yet he who is least in the kingdom of heaven is greater than he" (Matthew 11:11). Perhaps Jesus was saying that the grace and salvation that he would win on the cross would make even the newly baptized baby in the Church of the new covenant greater than the last and greatest prophet of the Old Testament, John the Baptist.

However, if Catholics were to choose among the saints of the new covenant, many would claim that the greatest of them was the first person to experience fully the saving power of the grace that Jesus won on the cross: his mother, Mary. We will devote our next chapter to her role in God's plan of salvation.

Chapter Nine

Mary: Mother of God and Our Mother

Mary, the mother of Jesus, is seen either as one of God's greatest *gifts* to the Church or, because of the honor Catholics give her, as one of the greatest *obstacles* to understanding and accepting the Catholic (or Orthodox) faith. As faith in Jesus as the Son of God is a "stumbling block" to Jews and other non-Christians, Catholic beliefs about Mary are a stumbling block to some Christians.

So how do Catholics arrive at their beliefs about Mary? Why do Catholics lavish special honor and titles on her? Does this detract from the glory that ought to be given to God alone? Let's look at these and other questions about the mother of Jesus.

Why do Catholics honor Mary?

Catholics honor Mary because God has honored her. God has given Mary the highest honor that is possible for a human person. Are we speaking of the honor that God bestowed on her when he took human nature from her flesh and dwelt in her womb? No. When a woman cried out to Jesus, "Blessed is the womb that bore you, and the breasts that you sucked!" Jesus replied, "Blessed rather are those who hear the word of God and keep it!" (Luke 11:27–28).

We honor Mary above all because of her faith and total submission to God's will and plan. When the angel Gabriel appeared to her and announced that she was to be the mother of "the Son of the Most High," who would inherit the throne of King David and rule forever (Luke 1:30–33), Mary did not doubt, even though she was a virgin. She replied, "I am the handmaid [servant] of the Lord; let it be to me according to your word" (Luke 1:38). For this response of total faith, the Holy Spirit inspired her cousin Elizabeth to tell Mary, "Blessed is she who believed that there would be a fulfilment of what was spoken to her from the Lord" (Luke 1:45). The Lord honors Mary because she, above all people, heard the word of God and kept it.

After her cousin Elizabeth had praised her, Mary in turn directed all the praise and glory to God: "My soul magnifies the Lord, and my spirit rejoices in God my Savior,... for he who is mighty has done great things for me, and holy is his name" (Luke 1:46–47, 49). This great hymn of praise to God, Mary's Magnificat, expresses perfectly her heart and her attitude.

Do Catholics worship Mary? Shouldn't Christians pray to God alone?

These are two different questions, and it is important to understand why they are different. There is a difference between worshiping someone and praying to someone.

Catholics understand (with all other Christians) that only God is to be worshiped and adored. The first commandment is, "I am the LORD your God.... You shall have no other gods before me" (Exodus 20:2, 3). Mary is *not* a fourth member of the Blessed Trinity. She is not God but only a human being. Therefore Catholics do not worship Mary.

Catholics, however, do pray to Mary, which means that we can speak to Mary when we pray. As discussed in the previous chapter, Catholics believe we can speak to other saints in heaven as well. We all are fellow members of God's redeemed family, which Catholics call the communion of saints. Catholics believe that Mary has a very special place in this family of God, which includes those now living on earth and those united to God fully in heaven, as well as those being purified of sin in purgatory.

Every family has a mother. Catholics believe that Jesus gave Mary to all his followers to be our mother—the mother of all his faithful followers. Jesus, in fact, did this as one of his last acts before his death. He looked down from the cross and said to John, the "beloved disciple": "Behold, your mother!" (John 19:27).

Some people say that Jesus, in his words to Saint John, was only making sure that Mary would be cared for after he died. Yet anyone who has studied the Gospel of Saint John knows that this Gospel always speaks on two levels: the literal human level and the deeper spiritual level. In this case it is obvious that the apostle John was to take care of Mary after Jesus died, but on a deeper level Jesus was giving Mary to all his "beloved disciples" to be their spiritual mother.

Catholics, therefore, do not worship Mary. But we do see her as our mother, and we give her the special honor and love that children ought to give to their mother.

Where do Catholics get their beliefs about Mary?

Basically, Catholic beliefs about Mary come from the Bible and from prayer and reflection on what the Bible says about Mary and Jesus. Mary appears in the Bible at key points in the life of her son and of the Church. The Gospel of Luke records how the Son of God came into the world through Mary's yes to the archangel Gabriel's announcement that she would become the mother of Israel's Savior. This yes is called Mary's *fiat,* which means "Let it be done."

Luke's Gospel also recounts that Mary and Joseph presented Jesus in the temple in accordance with Jewish law. And when Jesus was twelve years old, they searched for him after he remained behind in Jerusalem to talk with the elders in the temple. The Bible portrays Mary as a woman of great faith but also as one who had the normal concerns of a mother.

Mary accepted the prophecy of Simeon that through her son "a sword will pierce through your own soul" (Luke 2:35). Mary would suffer with and through her son. She saw Jesus laughed at during his public ministry because he came from an insignificant town and was a carpenter's son. She saw the Pharisees, the leaders of God's people at that time, challenge his authority. She saw the crowds reject Jesus as his hour drew near.

And of course the greatest trial for Mary was following her son in his agonizing walk to Calvary and seeing him slowly die on that gruesome cross, all the while being mocked by soldiers, onlookers and even another criminal hanging next to Jesus. Michelangelo's famous sculpture the *Pietà* portrays Mary cradling Jesus' lifeless body after it was taken down from the cross.

Yes, Mary was with Jesus at every key moment of his

life, and she continued to follow him in the community of Jesus' disciples. The Church was born on the feast of Pentecost when Mary and all Jesus' followers were waiting in prayer, as Jesus had instructed them to do before he ascended to the Father in heaven. The Holy Spirit, who descended in power on Mary at the Annunciation, now came in power to *all* Jesus' followers—which is certainly what she was praying for!

What about prayers to Mary, like the Hail Mary and the rosary? Where do we find these in the Bible?

"Hail [Mary], full of grace, the Lord is with you!" This is the archangel Gabriel's greeting to Mary (Luke 1:28), and an angel is God's messenger, who speaks only the truth. When Mary visited her cousin Elizabeth, who also was with child—John the Baptist—Elizabeth was filled with the Holy Spirit, and she exclaimed with a loud cry: "Blessed are you among women, and blessed is the fruit of your womb [Jesus]!" (Luke 1:42).

So the first part of the Hail Mary is simply two Bible verses about Mary. The second part is just a request for Mary to pray for us and for the whole Church, as she did in the Upper Room before Pentecost (see Acts 1:12–14): "Holy Mary, Mother of God, pray for us sinners, now and at the hour of our death."

The rosary is a collection of ancient Christian prayers: the Apostles' Creed, the doxology or "Glory be to the Father...," the Our Father and the Hail Mary, all of which are found in or based on the New Testament. These prayers are arranged as a meditation of twenty "mysteries"—central events in the lives of Jesus and Mary.

The Joyful Mysteries (Jesus' conception, birth and childhood)

1. The Annunciation
2. The Visitation
3. The Nativity (the Birth of Jesus)
4. The Presentation in the Temple
5. The Finding of Jesus in the Temple

The Luminous Mysteries (Jesus' public ministry)

1. The Baptism of Jesus
2. The Wedding Feast at Cana
3. The Proclamation of the Kingdom of God and Call to Conversion
4. The Transfiguration
5. The Institution of the Eucharist (at the Last Supper)

The Sorrowful Mysteries (Jesus' passion and death)

1. The Agony in the Garden
2. The Scourging at the Pillar
3. The Crowning With Thorns
4. The Carrying of the Cross
5. The Crucifixion and Death of Jesus

The Glorious Mysteries (the exaltations of Jesus and Mary)

1. The Resurrection of Jesus
2. The Ascension of Jesus
3. The Descent of the Holy Spirit (on Pentecost)
4. The Assumption of Mary
5. The Crowning of Mary as Queen of Heaven

It is evident that these Catholic prayers and meditations are rooted in the Bible, though two or three come from prayerful reflection on what is in the Bible, as we will discuss shortly. In summary, when Catholics pray the Hail Mary or the rosary, they pray as the Bible gives example or specifically teaches Christians to pray.

What about the things Catholics believe about Mary that aren't in the Bible? How do we know they are true?

Remember that Catholics don't accept the presupposition that the Bible is the only source of God's revealed truth. (Nowhere does the Bible teach that *only* Scripture is inspired.) Some Catholic beliefs about Mary come from prayer and reflection on Scripture and are part of the Church's tradition. Note that no belief of the Church could ever contradict the true, sure meaning of sacred Scripture; God doesn't contradict himself. But God does teach us truth through the voice of both sacred Scripture (the Bible) and sacred Tradition. Let's look at some of these beliefs.

Why is Mary called "the Immaculate Conception," and why do Catholics believe this?

Really, all Catholic beliefs about Mary tell us as much about her son, Jesus, as they do about her. For example, from early times Mary was called *Theotokos,* which means "the one who bore God." We now say that Mary is the *Mother of God,* because the one she carried in her womb and gave birth to was God or, more specifically, the Second Person of God, who is God the Son. Because this Son or Word of God took his human nature from Mary, and because the Son whom she bore is God, Mary is rightly honored by the title Mother of God.

What does this have to do with the Immaculate Conception? This doctrine tells us that Mary herself was conceived immaculately—that is, conceived in her mother's womb without the slightest stain of sin, not even the original sin that every other human being (except Jesus, of course) has inherited from Adam and Eve.

Why was Mary conceived without sin? God knew that the Son of God would one day come to dwell in her body and take a human nature from her. Because God is all holy, God prepared Mary from the moment of her conception to be a spotless, pure vessel or *ark* (to use an Old Testament image; see Exodus 25:10–22) where God could dwell. Mary is the "Ark of the New Covenant" because she bore God in her womb.

Obviously, this was not anything that Mary could have earned or deserved. It was God's free gift, which reminds us that all salvation—freedom from sin and death—is God's free gift, which no one can earn or deserve.

Mary has been called the *second* Eve or the *new* Eve because she is the first woman since Eve to be born without stain of sin. And just as the first Eve was called "mother of all living" (Genesis 3:20), Mary, the new Eve, is the mother of all those who live by the grace of her son. Jesus was the first man to be conceived without sin, so he is the new or second Adam. He is the source of all grace and the model or prototype of the new, redeemed humanity (see 1 Corinthians 15:45). The Immaculate Conception of Mary and the birth of her sinless son are the beginning of a new humanity, a new start for the human race.

Does the Bible say anything about Mary's Immaculate Conception? The angel Gabriel declared Mary to be "full of grace" (Luke 1:28), and Elizabeth, inspired by the Holy Spirit, proclaimed her to be "blessed... among women" (Luke 1:42). Mary herself exalted in God's mercy toward her in her hymn of praise, the Magnificat: "Henceforth all generations will call me blessed; for he who is mighty has done great things for me, and holy is his name" (Luke 1:48–49).

The saints of the early Church, both East and West, understood this to mean that Mary was "free of every stain of sin."[1] She shone with radiance among women as "a lily among thorns."[2]

What do Christians in more recent times think about Mary's immaculate conception?

In more recent times even Martin Luther, founder of the Protestant Reformation, continued to honor Mary and to believe in her immaculate conception, even after he left the Catholic Church. Blessed Pope Pius IX in 1854 officially declared Mary's immaculate conception a belief that is infallibly true and therefore something that all should accept as Christian teaching or doctrine.

As a sort of divine confirmation, in 1858, four years after Pope Pius's definition, a beautiful lady appeared to a simple young peasant girl, Bernadette Soubirous, in Lourdes, France, and told her, "I am the Immaculate Conception." Bernadette had never heard of this title, but she repeated it to a trusted friend.

The Catholic Church accepts this appearance of Mary as a valid "private revelation," and hundreds of medically verified miraculous healings that have occurred at Lourdes over the past 150 years seem to verify this judgment. Many Catholics and others see Mary's words at Lourdes as a sign from God confirming that Mary was conceived without original sin. The Americas are dedicated to the prayers and protection of Mary under the title of the Immaculate Conception.

Mary is sometimes called "ever-Virgin" or "the Blessed Virgin Mary." What do Catholics believe about Mary's virginity?

The archangel Gabriel made it clear that Mary conceived Jesus by the power of the Holy Spirit, and Mary confirmed that she never had sexual relations (see Luke 1:34). When her betrothed, Joseph, found out that Mary was pregnant, his first thought was to send her away quietly, since they were not yet married and she had not conceived this child through Joseph (Matthew 1:18–19). Fortunately, an angel appeared to Joseph in a dream and explained the truth about Jesus' virginal conception (Matthew 1:20).

When Joseph married Mary, he did not have relations with her "until" (some biblical translations say) she had borne a son (see Matthew 1:25). The Greek word translated "until" might better be translated "before." Matthew's Gospel emphasizes the fact that Mary was indeed a virgin at the time Jesus was born. There is no necessary implication that Joseph and Mary had sexual contact after that.

Some Bible texts refer to the "brothers and sisters" of Jesus (see Matthew 12:46; Mark 3:31; 6:3; Luke 8:19), but the word used in these passages referred to all close relatives, such as cousins.

The Christian people have always believed that Mary remained a virgin throughout her life. She alone of all women bore the Son of God in her womb. In fact, the greatest teachers of the Church, from at least the fourth century on, spoke of Mary as having remained a virgin throughout her life. Those who proclaimed Mary's perpetual virginity include some of the most illustrious Christians of all time: Athanasius, Epiphanius, Jerome, Augustine, Cyril of Alexandria and others. One of the early Church councils, the Second Council of Constantinople (AD 553–554), twice referred to Mary as "ever-virgin." Even the Protestant reformers Martin Luther, John Calvin and Huldrych Zwingli affirmed their belief in Mary's perpetual virginity.

Mary's virginity does not demean sex within marriage. Mary and Joseph freely chose to honor God for the incredible gift of his choice to dwell within Mary. Her virginity is a sign of her total dedication to God. Her virginity affirms that she is truly the holy temple where God chose to live among men.

Why do Catholics believe that Mary was "assumed" (taken up) into heaven?

All Catholic beliefs about Mary are interconnected, and all are related to Jesus Christ. We have discussed how Mary was conceived without sin and how she consecrated herself totally to God. This included her virginity and her sinlessness throughout her life: Mary always chose to do God's will.

Death is a consequence of sin. Since Mary was without sin, Catholics believe (based on the testimony and tradition of the early Church) that "having completed the course of her earthly life, [she] was assumed body and soul to heavenly glory."[3] This was the statement of Pope Pius XII when he formally defined this doctrine in 1950.

Mary's assumption into heaven shows the result of her freedom from sin. The end of the life of Mary, the new Eve, shows what might have happened to Adam and Eve had they not sinned. It also foreshadows what will happen to each faithful Christian one day, when the body is resurrected and comes into the glory of God in heaven. Mary goes before us to show us the way—both in her life on earth and at the end of her life.

After her assumption into heaven, Mary, the most humble person on earth, was lifted up to the highest place in heaven. This was after the pattern of her son, Jesus, who "humbled himself and became obedient unto death" (Philippians 2:8). Because of this "God has highly exalted him and bestowed on him the name which is above every name" (Philippians 2:9). God exalted Jesus, his Son, with the highest name; just so, God lifted up his mother Mary. She has received in heaven the fulfillment of the words of the Magnificat: "He has put down the mighty from their thrones, and exalted those of low degree" (Luke 1:52).

Catholics see Mary as the woman spoken of in the book of Revelation: "And a great sign appeared in heaven, a woman clothed with the sun, with the moon under her feet, and on her head a crown of twelve stars" (Revelation 12:1). This is the woman who "brought forth a male child, one who is to rule all the nations" (Revelation 12:5).

Jesus, in John's Gospel, twice addresses his mother as "woman" (see John 2:4; 19:26). Who could this glorified woman be—clothed with the sun and crowned with twelve stars—but Mary, the mother of the child who is destined to rule all the nations? Truly Jesus has exalted her, the lowly servant of the Lord, to be the queen of heaven!

I can understand honoring Mary, but why do Catholics pray to her? Why not just pray to Jesus or to God the Father, as Jesus taught us?

First, it is important to remember that Catholics understand God the Father as the Father of a great family, the communion of saints—all those united to God in love. In this family we speak to one another—sometimes honoring each other, sometimes asking for help or support. When we speak to saints who have died and are in the glory of heaven, this is a form of prayer, but it is not worship, which is due to God alone. Rather we join the saints and Mary in glorifying and worshiping God, the source of all good, the fullness of power, beauty and truth.

Second, we believe that when we honor the saints, we honor God. If a king chooses to raise up a queen, his subjects honor the king when they honor the queen. We believe Jesus has chosen to raise up Mary to be his queen (as well as his earthly mother). In honoring Mary we are recognizing and honoring one whom God has honored, and so we are honoring God.

Third, when Christians have a need, they certainly can and should pray to God. Jesus told us that the Father loves us and desires to give his children good things when they ask (see Matthew 7:11). However, part of the dynamic of a family is that sometimes we ask our siblings and, especially, our mother to intercede for us with the father of the family.

When we ask Mary, Jesus' mother and our heavenly mother, to intercede or to mediate for us with God, this is not only natural and human but also biblical: Mary was the one who went to Jesus for help on behalf of the couple at the wedding at Cana. Even though Jesus said that the "hour" for revealing his power had not yet come, at Mary's request he changed the water into wine for the wedding feast (see John 2:1–11). Thus, when we ask Mary to intercede for us and, in the Hail Mary, to "pray for us sinners now and at the hour of our death," we are doing something good that is rooted in the Bible.

How would you summarize the role of Mary in God's plan?

Mary's role could be summed up in five words beginning with the letter m:

- *Member* of the Church. This reminds us that Mary is not God nor a goddess but a person like us, who is a part of God's people.

- *Model* for all Christians. Mary lived her whole life in perfect obedience to God, by faith in God, wholeheartedly responding to God's grace and call. She is a model of discipleship (following Jesus), a model of faith and a model of the Church, expressing all that God calls the Church to be and to do.

- *Mother* of all Christians. As we have seen, Mary was not just the earthly mother of Jesus, but God has made her a spiritual mother of all who follow Jesus Christ. The beloved disciple John was the first to receive her in this role (see John 19:27).

- *Mediatrix* of grace. A mediatrix or mediator is one who intercedes on behalf of another. This role of Mary flows from her spiritual motherhood. As the spiritual mother of all who follow Christ, Mary continues to pray and to intercede to God for all her children—all God's people. Mary affirms and says yes to all the blessings and graces that God pours out.

  The Second Vatican Council explained that Mary's mediation in no way conflicts with the unique mediation of her son, Jesus, whom Scripture calls the "one mediator between God and men" (1 Timothy 2:5). Just as Jesus is the one "great high priest" (Hebrews 4:14), he enables us to share in his priesthood as his priestly people (see 1 Peter 2:9). In the same way, when we intercede for one another, and in a special way when Mary, our mother, intercedes for us, Jesus Christ gives his people a share in his role of mediation. All of us, including Mary, always approach the Father through Jesus. Jesus said, "No one comes to the Father, but by me" (John 14:6).

- *Messenger.* Catholics believe that at key points in history, Jesus has sent Mary to proclaim some aspect of the gospel that needs to be heard. In 1531 Mary appeared in Guadalupe, Mexico, to a peasant, Saint Juan Diego. This appearance led to the conversion of six to eight million native people to Jesus Christ.

I have mentioned Mary's appearance in more recent times to Saint Bernadette at Lourdes, France, affirming her title of the Immaculate Conception. Mary also appeared at Fatima, Portugal, in 1917, where she called the world to repent and to pray for peace and for the conversion of Russia. She recommended the rosary as a particularly powerful means of prayer.

Even though these appearances of Mary are private revelations, they are signs that God continues to speak to us and to express his care and love for his people through our mother Mary.

Chapter Ten

The Last Stop:
Our Destiny in Christ

In the *Star Wars* movie *The Return of the Jedi,* Luke Skywalker's father tells him that it is Luke's destiny to follow in his footsteps by rejecting good and turning to evil (the "dark side"). Fortunately, Darth Vader was wrong. Christianity too teaches that our destiny is not a fate beyond our control. We can and must choose our ultimate destiny.

The choices we make during our lives will be brought to light. "For we shall all stand before the judgment seat of God.... Each of us shall give account of himself to God" (Romans 14:10, 12). "We make it our aim to please him [the Lord]. For we must all appear before the judgment seat of Christ, so that each one may receive good or evil, according to what he has done in the body" (2 Corinthians 5:9–10).

What does Christianity teach about death?

Christians understand that our life on earth is a fleeting moment and a preparation for eternal life and the things to come—death and judgment, leading to heaven or hell. We should not be fearful or anxious in confronting these last things. Jesus Christ has conquered sin and death and has revealed the truth about the eternal destiny of the human race.

Jesus said, "I am the resurrection and the life; he who believes in me, though he dies, yet shall he live" (John 11:25). He responded to some Sadducees, "who say there is no resurrection": "As for the resurrection of the dead, have you not read what was said to you by God, 'I am the God of Abraham, and the God of Isaac, and the God of Jacob'? He is not God of the dead, but of the living" (Matthew 22:31–32). Luke's Gospel adds, "For all live to him" (Luke 20:38).

A "live demonstration" of this teaching occurred when Jesus went up Mount Tabor with Peter, James and John. Suddenly they saw him talking with Moses and Elijah, who were not dead but very much alive (see Matthew 17:1–3; Mark 9:2–4)!

The apostle Paul wrote:

> "Death is swallowed up in victory."
> "O death, where is your victory?
> O death, where is your sting?"
> The sting of death is sin, and the power of sin is the law. But thanks be to God, who gives us the victory through our Lord Jesus Christ.
> Therefore, my beloved brethren, be steadfast, immovable, always abounding in the work of the Lord, knowing that in the Lord your labor is not in vain. (1 Corinthians 15:54–58)

Christians look forward to death with hope in Jesus Christ, our Victor over sin and death.

What is heaven?

Heaven is eternal life with God. It is the goal of human existence, the purpose for which God created all humanity.

Genesis reveals that God's original plan was to unite all of humanity with him in everlasting life. Sin disrupted this plan. Human beings became subject to physical death and to hell, the ultimate death of eternal separation from God. Yet God mercifully restored his plan of life for all people through his Son, Jesus Christ. As the Gospel of John tells us, "For God so loved the world that he gave his only-begotten Son, that whoever believes in him should not perish but have eternal life" (John 3:16).

Saint Paul emphasizes that God's love and desire for salvation extend to all people:

> [God] desires all men to be saved and to come to the knowledge of the truth. For there is one God, and there is one mediator between God and men, the man Christ Jesus, who gave himself as a ransom for all....
>
> We have our hope set on the living God, who is the Savior of all men, especially of those who believe. (1 Timothy 2:4–6; 4:10)

Jesus Christ is the Son of God, the one mediator between God and humanity and the firstborn of a new creation (see Colossians 1:15–20). Jesus is the founder of a new race of men and women who are no longer destined to die but who will live eternally with God in heaven.

What will heaven be like?

The New Testament describes heaven as a joyous wedding feast (see Matthew 22:1–14; 25:1–13) and a great banquet (Luke 14:16–24) that will last forever. The book of

Revelation describes heaven as the marriage of the Lamb, Jesus Christ, to his bride, the Church (Revelation 19:7–9).

The ultimate glory of heaven will be the joy of seeing God and being perfectly transformed into his image. "At present we see indistinctly, as in a mirror, but then face to face. At present I know partially; then I shall know fully as I am fully known" (1 Corinthians 13:12, *NAB*). Catholics traditionally have called this face-to-face encounter with God in heaven "the beatific vision," the vision of God that brings perfect happiness.

These biblical images clearly proclaim that heaven is real. Some human beings will live forever in the joy of God's presence.

Who will attain the life of heaven? How many people will be there?

Catholic Christians believe that God does not satisfy our curiosity about such questions. The book of Revelation speaks of 144,000 elect, but this is a symbolic figure suggesting the perfect number (twelve times twelve times a thousand). Rather than speculate about who or how many will be in heaven, the Catholic Church emphasizes that we should follow the exhortation of Jesus: "Strive to enter by the narrow door; for many, I tell you, will seek to enter and will not be able" (Luke 13:24). Or as Paul urged: "Work out your own salvation with fear and trembling; for God is at work in you, both to will and to work for his good pleasure" (Philippians 2:12–13).

Two things are certain:

- First, nobody just drifts into heaven. Our final eternal destiny—heaven or hell—depends on the choices we make in this life, choices that deserve either eternal reward or eternal punishment.

- Second, no one enters heaven except by the grace of Jesus Christ, the one Savior of the world. Jesus said, "I am the way, and the truth, and the life; no one comes to the Father, but by me" (John 14:6).

What is hell?

God *desires* that all people be saved, but Jesus clearly warned that not everyone *will* be:

> Enter by the narrow gate; for the gate is wide and the way is easy, that leads to destruction, and those who enter by it are many. For the gate is narrow and the way is hard, that leads to life, and those who find it are few. (Matthew 7:13–14)

In the parables in which Jesus compared heaven to a wedding feast, a banquet and a harvest, he also stressed that not everyone will be gathered into the fulfilled kingdom. Some will be expelled to the outer darkness, where men will "weep and gnash their teeth" and the "chaff" will be burned with "unquenchable fire," "where their worm does not die, and the fire is not quenched" (Matthew 3:12; 8:12; Mark 9:48; Luke 3:17). These are the images of what the Bible calls hell (see Matthew 18:8–9; Mark 9:46–48), the state of eternal punishment and separation from God. The apostles and the early Church didn't make up hell. Jesus clearly taught that hell was real (Luke 16:19–31), and he implied that many people would end up there (Matthew 24:40–41).

Hell is an unpopular concept today, and some modern theologians question its existence or suggest that very few people actually go there. The teaching of the Catholic Church, however, is that hell does exist and that those who refuse to believe in Jesus, or who live in opposition to God and his will, will be condemned there in eternal separation from God. The apostle Paul warned those who emphasized the mercy and love of God to the neglect of his justice:

> Do you presume upon the riches of his kindness and forbearance and patience? Do you not know that God's kindness is meant to lead you to repentance? But by your hard and impenitent heart you are storing up wrath for yourself on the day of wrath when God's righteous judgment will be revealed. For he will render to every man according to his works: to those who by patience in well-doing seek for glory and honor and immortality, he will give eternal life; but for those who are factious and do not obey the truth, but obey wickedness, there will be wrath and fury. (Romans 2:4–8)

What will hell be like?

As with heaven, we do not fully comprehend what hell will be like, but all of the biblical images suggest that it is a place of darkness and torment (see Matthew 25:30; Luke 16:28), fire (Matthew 18:9; 13:30), wrath and fury (Romans 2:8). Hell is not a place where anyone would wish to visit, much less spend eternity!

Perhaps the greatest pain of those who are condemned to hell is their hopeless awareness that they are forever separated from God and their knowledge that they are responsible for having brought this fate upon themselves. For as John's Gospel makes clear, Jesus did not come to condemn but to save. Those who freely reject Jesus and his word condemn themselves by their own free decisions (see John 3:17–21; 12:47–48; also Matthew 12:36–37; Luke 19:10).

What is purgatory?

Scripture and Christian tradition undoubtedly affirm that heaven and hell exist, but what about that mysterious third state that Catholics and some other Christians call *purgatory*? The term itself is not found in the Bible, but the same may be said of other important Christian terms, such as the *Trinity* and the *Incarnation*.

God is constantly at work throughout our lives to purge us of sin. Catholics believe that God can complete this purifying work after a person's death. There are those who on earth have been oriented toward God and his will and who are not in serious rebellion against God—in a state of mortal sin—yet die with some venial (not deadly) sin or the effects of such sin still holding them back from full union with God. When they die they will go to purgatory for their final purification before entering heaven, where "you …must be perfect, as your heavenly Father is perfect" (Matthew 5:48).

Purgatory is not a second chance for salvation for those who have rejected God or have lived evil lives. Neither is it a "safety net" for people who hope that God will overlook serious sin in their lives if they die unrepentant. Rather, purgatory is a sign of God's mercy toward those who have honestly sought to know God and to do his will yet die in some degree of bondage to sin or the effects of sin.

God hates sin, and he would be perfectly just in condemning anyone bound by even the slightest sin or sin's effects at the time of death. Instead Catholics believe that

God chooses to purify repentant sinners, even after death, so that they can enter into the full joy of heaven.

Is purgatory necessary? Don't the merits of Jesus Christ's death suffice for the total remission of sin?

The answer to this last question is yes, all sin is totally forgiven and removed through the passion, death and resurrection of Jesus Christ. Catholic Christians understand purgatory as a way that this salvation in Jesus actually happens or is applied to individual persons. If a person dies in some bondage to sin or has been crippled by sin's effects, this sin and its effects must be removed, forgiven and purged before the person sees God face-to-face. Why? Because of God's holiness.

Sin and God are diametrically opposed. God is so pure, so holy, that nothing impure or sinful can enter into his presence (see Revelation 21:27). In purgatory God's holiness, his anger toward sin and his love of the repentant sinner burn away the remaining sin in the soul, "for our God is a consuming fire" (Hebrews 12:29). The person is drawn nearer to God and finally drawn into the full glory of his presence.

Does the Bible teach that nothing sinful can come into union with God?

Some biblical texts indicate this understanding of God's holiness and the purging from sin. The Hebrew people of the old covenant knew God's awesome holiness. They believed that if a person were to come directly into God's presence, he would die. Moses boldly asked God to "show me your glory" (Exodus 33:18), but God told Moses, "You cannot see my face; for man shall not see me and live"

(Exodus 33:20). God then hid Moses in the cleft of a rock and allowed Moses to see only his back after he had passed by. Elijah had a similar experience (see 1 Kings 19:9–13).

The prophet Isaiah had a vision of God upon a throne, with the angels surrounding him and crying, "Holy, holy, holy is the LORD of hosts" (Isaiah 6:3). Isaiah's immediate response was, "Woe is me!…For I am a man of unclean lips…; for my eyes have seen…the LORD of hosts!" (Isaiah 6:5). The Lord sent an angel to purify Isaiah's lips with a burning coal from the altar of God. "And he touched my mouth, and said, 'Behold, this has touched your lips; your guilt is taken away, and your sin forgiven'" (Isaiah 6:7). Only then was Isaiah able to speak the word of God to the people.

Isaiah's experience relates to the doctrine of purgatory. When people come before God in reality (not just in a vision), they will see their sin as it really is—ugly and detestable—and cry out, "Woe is me!" But for those who have spent their lives seeking God and striving to do his will, God in his mercy will send the fire of his love to purify them from their sin, so they can stand before him joyfully to praise him forever.

OK, the Old Testament gives some evidence for purgatory, but what does the New Testament teach about it?

Catholic Christians believe that the New Testament affirms the reality of purgatory. Saint Paul writes:

> For no other foundation can any one lay than that which is laid, which is Jesus Christ. Now if any one builds on the foundation with gold, silver, precious stones, wood, hay, straw—each man's work will become manifest; for the Day will disclose it, because it will be revealed with

> fire, and the fire will test what sort of work each one has
> done. If the work which any man has built on the foun-
> dation survives, he will receive a reward. If any man's
> work is burned up, he will suffer loss, though he himself
> will be saved, but only as through fire. (1 Corinthians
> 3:11–15)

This passage speaks about those who have built their lives
on the foundation of Jesus Christ. When these people are
judged, what they have done in this life will be tested. If it
is good, they will be rewarded. If their work is inferior—
sinful—the fire of judgment will burn it up. These people
will "suffer loss," although they will be saved, "but only as
through fire."

Christians in the early Church who reflected on this
passage came to believe that a purification by fire—a
purgatory—would come upon Christians whose lives and
works were imperfect in God's sight, although they themselves would be saved. In the fourth century Saint Gregory
of Nyssa wrote that "after his departure out of the body [a
soul that is not purified]...he is not able to partake of
divinity, until he has been purged of the filthy contagion in
his soul by the purifying fire."[1]

The image of fire shows that this purgation is painful
yet also cleansing and purifying. This is not an unfamiliar
idea: Even in this life we experience pain when God breaks
us from patterns of sin, yet we also experience healing and
liberation.

Should we pray for those who have died? What good does it do?

Those who have died, and certainly baptized Christians
who have died believing in Jesus Christ, are still part of

God's family. As we have seen, the communion of saints includes both the living and the dead.

Praying for the dead makes sense only if those prayers can benefit the dead. If the deceased have already arrived at their final destiny—heaven or hell—then praying for them would be futile. However, if the deceased are undergoing the healing and purification of purgatory, then prayer for God's mercy is reasonable and fitting. It is safe and right to assume that anyone who has died may be in need of the support of our prayers.

Prayer for the dead became a common practice in the early Church because the Christians believed that the Holy Spirit had led them to do this, based on their understanding of humanity's destiny after death. The early Christians believed that their prayers, calling on God's mercy, could hasten God's work of purifying and purging their deceased relatives and friends from sin. Inscriptions in the Roman catacombs indicate that Christians honored and prayed for their dead loved ones. Around AD 211 Tertullian wrote that Christians offered prayer and the Eucharist for the deceased on the anniversaries of their death.[2]

The list of the great fathers of the early Church who encouraged Christians to pray for the dead is impressive: Tertullian, Origen, Cyprian, Ambrose, Augustine, Basil, Gregory of Nazianzus, John Chrysostom, Pope Gregory the Great and many others. The ancient liturgies of the Church included powerful prayers for the dead, such as the beginning of this prayer from the liturgy of Saint John Chrysostom: "Let us pray also for the repose of the souls of the departed servants of God and for the forgiveness of their every transgression, deliberate and indeliberate."[3]

The Second Vatican Council reaffirmed this practice: "Very much aware of the bonds linking the whole Mystical Body of Jesus Christ, the pilgrim Church from the very first ages of the Christian religion has cultivated with great piety the memory of the dead. Because it is 'a holy and wholesome thought to pray for the dead that they may be loosed from sins' (2 Mach. 12:46), she has also offered prayers for them" (Constitution on the Church, 50).[4]

What will happen to purgatory at the end of time?

Catholic Christians believe that purgatory is a temporary state. When the Lord Jesus comes again in majesty, purgatory will come to an end, as will life on earth as we know it. The purification of those in purgatory and on earth will be completed in the Last Judgment. Then only two states will remain: heaven and hell.

What will happen at the end of human history?

The Bible and Christian tradition have given many names to the time when the glorified Jesus will return to judge all people and to bring human history to a close: the Day of the Lord, the *parousia,* the end times and the second coming of Christ. Some Christians believe that the Second Coming will inaugurate a thousand-year reign of Christ on earth, often called the "millennium" (see Revelation 19—20).

Catholic Christians usually have followed Saint Augustine's interpretation of this text about a thousand years. To him the thousand years (which is a biblical way of saying "a very long time") represents the whole history of the Church—from the sending of the Holy Spirit at Pentecost until Christ's return at the end of time. It is a time of God's victory but also a time of conflict. Jesus

Christ won the victory by his death on the cross, and yet Satan and his demons are still at work in the world, warring against the Church.

As this period of history closes, Satan's power will increase until Jesus comes to earth again and condemns him and his followers to eternity in hell, or the "lake of fire" (Revelation 20:10, 14). Followers of Jesus, whose names are written in the "book of life," will then enter forever into the "new Jerusalem" of heaven (see Revelation 21).

What will the Second Coming of Christ be like?

The Catholic Church always has affirmed and proclaimed certain biblical truths about the second coming of Jesus. The first basic truth is that Jesus will return to earth as the glorified "Son of Man" (see Daniel 7:13–14) to judge all of humanity and bring human history to an end (Matthew 25:31–46; Mark 13:26–27; Acts 1:11; 1 Corinthians 15:22–23; 1 Thessalonians 4:16–17; 2 Timothy 4:8; James 5:7–9). Nearly all of these biblical texts use bold, vivid images, called apocalyptic or revelational images, to describe the Second Coming. For example, in 1 Thessalonians 4:16–17, Paul speaks of archangel voices, the "trumpet of God" and people "caught up...in the clouds to meet the Lord in the air," an event some Christians call "the rapture."

Are the images of the Second Coming to be taken literally?

Many biblical scholars confidently affirm that the apocalyptic images are poetic images that help God's people envision what the Second Coming could be like. Other Christians firmly believe that these images are a literal description of the Second Coming. To my knowledge, the Catholic Church has never made any official statement on this question. This is wise, because no one will know whether the biblical images are poetic or literal until the Second Coming actually happens!

Rather than becoming entangled in arguments about this point, Catholic Christians prefer to focus on the basic truths contained in these passages, those on which everyone can agree:

- The first basic truth is that Jesus will return to earth as the glorious Son of Man to bring human history to an end and to judge all humankind. Catholic Christians profess in the Creed, "He will come again in glory to judge the living and the dead," and we proclaim in the Mass, "Christ has died, Christ is risen, Christ will come again!"

- The second basic truth, related to the first, is that the Second Coming of Christ will be unmistakable because unprecedented signs in the heavens and on earth will accompany it. "For as the lightning comes from the east and shines as far as the west, so will be the coming of the Son of man" (Matthew 24:27). Many people have fallen for false messiahs (saviors) and prophets over the centuries and continue to do so today. But Catholic Christians believe that Jesus is the only Lord, the only Messiah, the only Savior, and that his coming again to earth will be clear and unmistakable.

What signs will precede the Second Coming?

The Bible indicates that the signs preceding the parousia fall roughly into two categories.

The first are certain preliminary events that will occur sometime before Jesus' coming again. Matthew 24:14 teaches: "And this gospel of the kingdom will be preached throughout the whole world, as a testimony to all nations; and then the end will come." Paul, in his Letter to the Romans, speaks of the conversion of Israel to Christ after the "full number" of gentiles has been converted (see Romans 11:25–32). Catholic and Protestant Scripture scholars have interpreted these passages in various ways, but most agree that they refer to the worldwide evangelization that will precede the Second Coming of Christ.

The second category of signs is *proximate* signs. These signs employ vivid apocalyptic images from the Old Testament and other ancient literature. They are found especially in Mark 13, Matthew 24 and Luke 21.

For example, the synoptic Gospels report that there will be a period of great tribulation or trial immediately before Christ's return. This trial will be characterized by confusion and disorder in the world, in the Church and even in the physical condition of the earth and the heavens. Many will depart from the true Christian faith (see 1 Timothy 4:1–2) and will lead increasingly self-centered and debauched lives (2 Timothy 3:1–8), causing the love of many people to grow cold (Matthew 24:12). The Bible also tells of the rise of an Antichrist, an evil person or power trying to destroy the work of God on earth and the reign of Jesus Christ (2 Thessalonians 2:3–10; 1 John 2:18–23; 4:1–5; Revelation 20:7–8).

How does the Catholic Church interpret these signs of the Second Coming?

There is little official Catholic teaching about how to understand these signs, because the Catholic Church wants people to avoid pointless speculation about the identity of the Antichrist and the nature of the tribulation. However, the Church encourages people to take seriously the basic teaching of the Bible.

Christians should expect a time of extreme difficulty immediately before the glorious coming of Jesus Christ, accompanied by unprecedented signs in the heavens and on earth. The spiritual darkness of this world will grow even darker for those who have not acknowledged and believed in the Light and Savior of the world, Jesus Christ. There also will be signs of the light of Christ shining more brightly in the world, as the gospel is proclaimed to all the nations, and many are converted to Christ.

Will Jesus come at a time we expect, or will his coming be sudden and unexpected?

Another basic truth about the Second Coming of Christ is that no one knows exactly when it will happen. According to Jesus' teaching and parables, it will be sudden and unexpected, catching many people unprepared. The exact time of Jesus' return is not ours to know, and the attempts of many Christians today and throughout the centuries to predict it are in vain.

Jesus said that even he did not know the exact time of his Second Coming: "But of that day or that hour no one knows, not even the angels in heaven, nor the Son, but only the Father" (Mark 13:32). Nearly every biblical scholar today believes this is an actual saying of Jesus, because it is one of the rare times in the Gospels in which Jesus claims to be ignorant of something. The Gospel writers would certainly not have conceded that Jesus didn't know something unless he actually claimed that he didn't.

Further, the parables of Jesus emphasize that the coming of the Lord will be sudden and unexpected. Matthew's Gospel records four consecutive parables in which Jesus warns his followers about how unexpected his coming again will be (see Matthew 24:36—25:13). A favorite biblical image is that the end will come like a "thief": Paul uses this image in 1 Thessalonians 5:2; Peter uses it in 2 Peter 3:10; and it is also in Matthew's Gospel (24:43). The point, of course, is that just as no one knows when a thief will break in, no one knows exactly when Christ will come again.

Catholic Christians do not claim to know any more than Jesus or the Bible on this topic, and so we avoid speculating about how or when the end will come. The Church does teach that Christians always should be prepared for the Second Coming and should look forward to it with expectation. In Mark's Gospel, immediately after Jesus denied knowledge of the time of his Second Coming, he taught:

> Take heed, watch and pray; for you do not know when the time will come.... Watch therefore—for you do not know when the master of the house will come, in the evening, or at midnight, or at cockcrow, or in the morning—lest he come suddenly and find you asleep. And what I say to you I say to all: Watch! (Mark 13:33, 35–37)

How do Christians watch for the Second Coming of Jesus?

First, they are to prepare for his coming by leading *holy and upright lives.* Peter insisted on this in his two letters:

> Therefore gird up your minds, be sober, set your hope fully upon the grace that is coming to you at the revelation of Jesus Christ. As obedient children, do not be conformed to the passions of your former ignorance, but as he who called you is holy, be holy yourselves in all your conduct. (1 Peter 1:13–15)

> But do not ignore this one fact, beloved, that with the Lord one day is as a thousand years, and a thousand years as one day. The Lord is not slow about his promise as some count slowness, but is forbearing toward you, not wishing that any should perish, but that all should reach repentance. But the day of the Lord will come like a thief, and then the heavens will pass away with a loud noise, and the elements will be dissolved with fire, and the earth and the works that are upon it will be burned up.
>
> Since all these things are thus to be dissolved, what sort of persons ought you to be in lives of holiness and godliness, waiting for and hastening the coming of the day of God, because of which the heavens will be kindled and dissolved, and the elements will melt with fire! (1 Peter 3:8–12)

One way to hasten the coming of the Lord is to *pray for it.* This is a second attitude that Christians should have toward the parousia. One of the oldest Christian prayers is "Maranatha"—"Come, Lord!"

The third way that Christians should approach the Second Coming of Jesus Christ is to *look forward to it with joyous expectation.* The Second Coming will be a time of glory and reward for all of Jesus' faithful followers. "For God is not so unjust as to overlook your work and the love which you showed for his sake in serving the saints, as you still do" (Hebrews 6:10).

Saint Paul wrote words of encouragement to the Christians in Thessalonica:

> For you are all sons of light and sons of the day; we are not of the night or of darkness. So then let us not sleep, as others do, but let us keep awake and be sober.... For God has not destined us for wrath, but to obtain salvation through our Lord Jesus Christ, who died for us so that whether we wake or sleep we might live with him. (1 Thessalonians 5:5–6, 9–10)

Do Catholics and other Christians need to be anxious or fearful about the end of the world and the Last Judgment?

Christians who have believed in Christ and who have lived their lives in the light of his presence should have no fear of the Day of Judgment. As long as we do not fall into the darkness of sin, we have confident hope of salvation. Jesus himself instructed his disciples, "Now when these things [the signs immediately preceding the Second Coming] begin to take place, look up and raise your heads, because your redemption is drawing near" (Luke 21:28).

Christians can look forward with confidence to obtaining eternal life with God through the merits of the death and resurrection of Jesus Christ our Savior and by the power of the Holy Spirit. Christians realize, with Saint Paul, that "this slight momentary affliction is preparing for us an eternal weight of glory beyond all comparison, because we look not to the things that are seen but to the things that are unseen; for the things that are seen are transient, but the things that are unseen are eternal" (2 Corinthians 4:17–18).

"Therefore let us be grateful for receiving a kingdom that cannot be shaken, and thus let us offer to God acceptable worship, with reverence and awe; for our God is a consuming fire" (Hebrews 12:28–29).

MARANATHA! COME, LORD JESUS!

Notes

Introduction

1. For a readable, comprehensive Catholic catechism based on
    and referenced to the official *Catechism of the Catholic
    Church,* I have written *The Essential Catholic Catechism*
    (Cincinnati: Servant, 1999). That book includes discussion
    of Catholic moral teaching, liturgy, prayer and other topics
    that this book does not address or only mentions.

2. Plato, *Apology of Socrates,* www.classics.mit.edu.

Chapter One: God and Man

1. Christians are thus "monotheists," believers in one God
    —as opposed to "polytheists," who believe in many gods;
    "atheists," who deny the existence of any god or supreme
    being; and "agnostics," who do not know whether there is a
    god or gods and who think that human beings can't know
    this for sure.

2. Some people think that God is the sum total of everything
    that exists: "everything" is God. These people are called
    "pantheists." Christians think that God is everywhere, since
    God is not limited and thus is present in everything, but
    that he is not to be confused with his creation, even though
    he is present in this creation.

Chapter Two: Salvation: God's Free Gift in Jesus Christ

1. This quote is from Walter Abbott, *Documents of Vatican II* (New York: America, 1966), p. 35.

Chapter Three: The Sources of Catholic Beliefs

1. Abbott, p. 118.

Chapter Four: The Church: God's Plan

1. *Lumen Gentium,* meaning "Light to the Nations," is the Latin title for the central document of Vatican II, The Dogmatic Constitution on the Church.

2. Pope John Paul II, Apostolic Letter *Novo Millennio Ineunte,* Vatican trans. (Boston: Daughters of St. Paul, 2001), pp. 16–17.

3. Abbott, p. 25.

4. See Augustine, *Treatise on Baptism* V, 27:38—28:39, quoted in Maurice Wiles and Mark Santer, eds., *Documents in Early Christian Thought* (London: Cambridge University Press, 1975), pp. 163–166.

5. Augustine, *Confessions,* bk. 9, chap. 10, in John K. Ryan, ed., *The Confessions of St. Augustine* (New York: Doubleday, 1960), p. 223.

6. See "The Letter of the Church of Rome to the Church of Corinth, Commonly Called Clement's First Letter," in Cyril R. Richardson, ed., *Early Christian Fathers* (New York: Macmillan, 1975), pp. 43–73; "The Letters of Ignatius, Bishop of Antioch," in Richardson, pp. 74–120.

Chapter Five: Leadership in the Church

1. *Didache,* 15:1–2, in Richardson, p. 178.

2. Ignatius, "Letter to the Smyrnaeans," in Richardson, p. 115.

3. Saint Irenaeus, "Against Heresies," in Richardson, p. 372.

Chapter Six: The Work of the Holy Spirit

1. Augustine of Hippo, Sermon 267, sec. 4, in William A.
   Jurgens, *The Faith of the Early Fathers* (Collegeville, Minn.:
   Liturgical, 1979), vol. 3, p. 31.

2. Augustine of Hippo, *The Trinity* (6, 5, 7), in Jurgens, vol. 3,
   p. 76.

3. Cyril of Jerusalem, Catechetical Lecture 16, "On the Holy
   Spirit," in *Liturgy of the Hours,* English ed., vol. 2
   (New York: Catholic Book, 1976), p. 968.

4. Pope John Paul II, *Crossing the Threshold of Hope*
   (New York: Knopf, 1994), p. 19.

5. ——, *Crossing the Threshold of Hope,* p. 16.

6. ——, "Christian Unity Is Gift of the Spirit," *L'Osservatore
   Romano,* January 27, 1993, English edition,
   p. 11. Italics are in the original.

7. Peter Kreeft, *Fundamentals of the Faith: Essays in
   Christian Apologetics* (San Francisco: Ignatius, 1988),
   p. 142.

8. See, for example, Raniero Cantalamessa, *Sober Intoxication
   of the Spirit: Filled with the Fullness of God,* Marsha
   Daigle-Williamson, trans. (Cincinnati: Servant, 2005).

9. For "new springtime" see Encyclical Letter of John Paul II,
   Mission of the Redeemer, Vatican trans. (Boston: St. Paul,
   1991), no. 86, p. 106; for "new evangelization" see *Mission of
   the Redeemer*, no. 3, p. 12: "I sense that the moment has
   come to commit all of the Church's energies to a new evangelization." Also see *Novo Millennio Ineunte,* no. 40, p. 52:
   "Over the years, I have often repeated the summons to the
   new evangelization. I do so again now.... We must rekindle
   in ourselves the impetus of the beginnings and allow ourselves to be filled with the ardor of the apostolic preaching
   which followed Pentecost."

Chapter Eight: The Saints: Our Friends in Glory

1. C.S. Lewis, *The Screwtape Letters* (New York: Macmillan, 1959), p. 12.

2. Saint Jerome, "Against Vigilantius," in Jurgens, vol. 2, p. 206.

3. Thérèse of Lisieux, *The Story of a Soul,* John Clarke, trans. (Washington: ICS, 1996), epilogue, p. 263.

4. Abbott, p. 82.

Chapter Nine: Mary: Mother of God and Our Mother

1. Ambrose of Milan, "Commentary on Psalm 118," 22, 30, in Jurgens, vol. 2, p. 166.

2. Edward D. O'Connor, "The Development of Marian Doctrine in the Church," *God's Word Today,* May 1982, p. 44.

3. Pope Pius XII, *Munificentissimus Deus,* quoted in Michael O'Carroll, *Theotokos: A Theological Encyclopedia of the Blessed Virgin Mary* (Wilmington, Del.: Glazier, 1982), p. 55.

Chapter Ten: The Last Stop: Our Destiny in Christ

1. Gregory of Nyssa, "Sermon on the Dead," in Jurgens, vol. 2, p. 58.

2. Tertullian, "The Crown" (3, 2) and "On Monogamy" (10, 1), in Jurgens, vol. 1, pp. 151 (no. 367), 158 (no. 382).

3. Quoted in George A. Maloney, *The Everlasting Now* (Notre Dame, Ind.: Ave Maria, 1980), p. 64.

4. Abbott, p. 81.

Index